# NEW WESTMINSTER SERMONS

Every blessing,
Martyn Atkins

MARTYN ATKINS

## DEDICATION

*To all at Methodist Central Hall, Westminster, with whom to spend the last five years of my ministry as a Methodist presbyter in Britain was a blessing for which I am hugely grateful.*

## ENDORSEMENTS

In this collection of sermons Martyn Atkins has managed to combine profound doctrine and missiology with ready accessibility for his readers. The sermons contain many illustrations that readers will easily relate to, and which help us all discern how God is at work in our own lives. The sermon 'Discipleship – Methodist Style' is a fine example of preached tradition, relevant scholarship and application, ably reminding Methodist Christians of the nature of discipleship of Christ. A fabulous read.

*Revd Loraine Mellor, President of the Methodist Conference 2017*

Martyn Atkins has a keen way of weaving together profound theology with ordinary life. Far from an aloof ivory tower academic, Martyn, a local church practitioner, brings the richness of the Christian faith into our everyday lives. These are messages from a good pastor to a great congregation in the heart of London that Martyn deeply loves and in whom he desires to see Christ formed. There is gold in these sermons to be mined by followers of Jesus.

*Jorge Acevedo, Lead Pastor: Grace Church (Florida USA), multi-site United Methodist congregation*

This book of sermons is exceptional. The warm style and clear reasoning in these vibrant messages brings refreshing insights to the great themes of Christianity. Martyn's love for the people at Methodist Central Hall, Westminster and theirs for him is evident in these pages, and his ministry amongst them as enriching as his sermons. Reading them, I have been brought to the feet of Jesus.

*Revd Steve Wild, President of the Methodist Conference 2015*

A catalogue record for this book is available from the British Library.

ISBN 978-0-85346-342-9

Design and typesetting by Joensuu Media Ltd

Printed by InDevelop in Latvia


Methodist Central Hall, Westminster
Storey's Gate, Westminster
London SW1H 9NH

# CONTENTS

The Christian Year

# FOREWORD

Preaching is both a spiritual gift and creative art – and Martyn Atkins has both in spades! This selection of sermons reveals the skill and art of crafting 'words about the Word' to shape a message, which goes to the heart of people's experience.

I first heard Martyn preach at Cliff College in 1995. I had invited him to lead Bible studies at the Derwent Week Convention that year. The studies, on encounters with the risen Jesus, were illuminating, with effortless scholarship, full of insight, related to real life and tempered by humour. He always had a captivating angle on the Bible passage with illustrations drawn from his wide scholarship, his life experience (which sadly includes supporting Leeds United Football Club), catering, ministry and family life. We get all that in these sermons.

These *New Westminster Sermons* are a gift which continues the Methodist legacy of Wesley and Sangster. Like the latter, these were all preached to the congregation at the Methodist Central Hall, Westminster. They cover key moments in the spiritual journey of people: finding faith, being baptised, conversion, confirmation and points of renewal. They identify significant dates in the Wesleyan calendar – the covenant service and Aldersgate Sunday – as well as seasons and festivals in the church year such as Advent, Lent, Easter and Pentecost. They become helpful guides for those of us preparing sermons as the seasons come around. Beware though, just preaching Atkins – make the ideas your own!

# NEW WESTMINSTER SERMONS

Whether you come to this collection as a person exploring faith or confident in faith, you will find in these sermons a challenge and signposts to a deepened faith. Preachers should read them once for themselves and then again to note how Martyn draws the reader, the hearer, into the subject, identifies the points with clarity and offers a challenge. There is always something to think about, to respond to, to engage with.

Mr Wesley directed his preachers to 'Offer Christ.' This is exactly what Martyn achieves in this collection of sermons.

*Revd Dr. G. Howard Mellor*

# INTRODUCTION

It might be thought odd or even presumptuous to publish a book of your own sermons! I would never have done so had not numerous people asked me for such a book. For a long time I resisted these requests, pointing out that many of these sermons are recorded and available on social media platforms, and surely watching and hearing a sermon is much better than reading one! Indeed, I've even sometimes posed the philosophical question whether a sermon written down is truly a sermon at all! Discuss! However, it was patiently pointed out to me that for many Christian people the reading of a sermon was of benefit, whether or not they had heard it. It permits time for reflection; you can go through the text at your own speed, ponder and pray. And after all, they said, isn't there a good Methodist tradition of published sermons? *John Wesley's Forty-four Sermons* for example, and of course *Westminster Sermons* by the great W. E. Sangster, Superintendent minister at Methodist Central Hall, Westminster (MCHW) between 1939 and 1955. In consequence, here it is, a selection of sermons preached over the five-year period I was myself privileged to be the Superintendent minister at MCHW. A far lesser and modest thing than those by my illustrious predecessors, yet humbly offered for the same purposes: Christian encouragement, teaching, inspiration and deepening discipleship of Christ.

Most preachers like to think their sermons are 'original' – though of course there's a doctrinal danger to them being so! I make no such claim here. Since I began preaching in 1973 I've probably heard thousands of sermons, addresses and lectures, and read hundreds of books and articles of many kinds. Add to this that I'm a compulsive notetaker with a relatively good memory and it probably means there's not an original thought between these covers! Consequently, if any readers, colleagues or friends recognise their own words, images or thoughts, I hope they're pleased rather than offended. When I'm consciously aware that I've borrowed from others I readily indicate that. In most instances I make brief introductory comments indicating indebtedness and the context in which the sermon was preached. In most cases the main readings used in the service are included.

Inevitably, there have been alterations while translating speech to text, but as few as possible, and my hope is that readers will be able to experience these as sermons, and to their benefit.

*Martyn Atkins*

# SEASONS OF DISCIPLESHIP
# AND SPECIAL OCCASIONS

# 1

# BELIEVE!

A sermon preached at a service including confirmation, church membership and the reaffirmation of baptismal promises using water – always a moving time of testimony and rejoicing.

Readings: Romans 10:9-13 & John 6:35-40.

*'If you declare with your mouth, "Jesus is Lord," and believe in your heart that God raised him from the dead, you will be saved…'* for, *'Everyone who calls on the name of the Lord will be saved.'* (Romans 10:9 & 13) In this joyful service I want to reflect on those words from our lesson from Romans.

*'If you declare with your mouth, "Jesus is Lord."'* 'Jesus is Lord' was the earliest creed of the Christian Church. It's written on the walls of the earliest catacombs of Christians in Rome. It's scratched into the floor of places thought to be ancient jails.

We can easily underestimate what 'Jesus is Lord' means – it trips off the tongue easily. But imagine being a slave at the time Romans was written and saying 'Jesus is Lord' – which puts everyone else into second place – including your 'owner'. That's dangerous. Or imagine being a soldier in the Roman army and saying 'Jesus is Lord,' which you know is regarded treason against the Emperor and punishable by death. Or imagine living in a country today that's ruled by a religion other than Christianity or a secular authority, where to declare 'Jesus is Lord' is outlawed or subversive, and puts your livelihood, or prospects of promotion, or the possibility of good schooling for your family – or even your life – at risk.

To declare 'Jesus is Lord' in this land today is relatively easy. Some might think you a bit odd, or a religious nut, but you don't run the risks of a slave, or a Roman soldier, or a Christian today living in Iran, Pakistan or Egypt, or parts of China.

What are we saying when we declare 'Jesus is Lord'? We're effectively saying the creeds. We're declaring that Jesus Christ, the Son of God born a human baby, who grew, taught and healed, who was arrested, beaten up and crucified, and who was raised from the dead and now lives for evermore, is the most important person in life.

To say 'Jesus is Lord' and mean it means that Jesus is in charge. What he wants goes. If Jesus is Lord, then he's in charge of our minds, and what we fill them with; our ethics, values, and how we live our lives, our career and future, our relationships and loved ones. To declare 'Jesus is Lord' is as if you'd stuck a big spiritual badge on your chest for all to see and it says, 'The property of Jesus Christ.' So that what you are, and who you are, and what you have actually belong to the Son of God. And do you know? If you think this sounds like repression or restriction, it's actually perfect freedom. Liberation. True delight. So don't be a secret, ashamed Christian. Declare that Jesus is Lord with your lips – and live out his lordship in your lives.

*'And believe in your heart that God raised him from the dead.'*

This is among the earliest beliefs of the Church. We shouldn't think this is the only thing we need to believe – that we needn't bother about whether or not Jesus was born, or died on the cross for our sins, and so on – that's not what this passage means. What it means is that from the earliest times Christians experienced Jesus to be alive. You see, Christianity isn't a faith based on a dead founder, a wonderful person who inspired many and taught great things, but died and is now remembered fondly. No. From the very beginning Christians proclaimed that God raised Christ from the dead. Which means that Jesus is alive and is a living Lord. And if a living Lord, then someone who is with you, and leads you, cares for you, loves you, now, today. As the old hymn goes, 'He lives, He lives, Christ Jesus lives today.'

It's the combination of confessing Jesus is Lord and believing God raised him from the dead that results, states the text, in our being saved. Now a possible problem is that we can interpret this to mean this is all there is to salvation. It's easy to be saved. Undemanding.

I wake up. Before I get out of bed I say 'Jesus is Lord' out loud, and I say to myself, 'I believe in my heart that God raised Jesus from the dead,' then I hop out of bed, job done. Saved. That's it. So I'll just hunker down, confident that God loves me and that I'm going to heaven when I die.

But I doubt we're meant to read these verses in such a superficial way. The book of Romans, written to communities of early Christians, some of whom were being ridiculed, threatened, or possibly persecuted for their faith, wants to reassure them that belief in Jesus Christ is not a mistake. That Jesus forgives sins and sets people free like nobody else can. That Jesus is right when he declares that God loves us, rather than despises us because of our sinfulness. That when we die we will go to heaven where there is everlasting joy and peace. That before we die we must live as Jesus wants us to. And all of that and more is being 'saved.' That's still the challenge to us today, and it is anything but superficial.

*'Everyone who calls on the name of the Lord will be saved.'*

The church in Rome wasn't perfect. Like cities everywhere there were the rich and poor, elites and beggars, landed gentry and homeless, masters and slaves, heroes and villains, establishment figures, rebels and outcasts. And there were many faiths

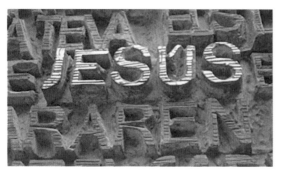

and many gods. The rich had their gods and said, 'If you can pay you can come into this temple. But if you can't, you can't come in.' Those of a certain birth or ethnicity thought themselves better than others – 'Only we can worship

*'Jesus' on the doors at La Sagrada Familia, H. Atkins*

here. You're different, you're not like us, so you can't.' Some religious groupings were only for men, and others only for women.

So we need to realise just how radical this statement in Romans is: 'Everyone who calls on the name of the Lord will be saved.' Because what the writer is doing is pointing out that the entry requirements for becoming Christian, for all their rigour, all their seriousness, are actually, wonderfully, open to all. 'If you declare with your mouth "Jesus is Lord," and believe in your heart that God raised him from the dead, you will be saved.' And be rich too, surely? No, that's not a condition. And be trueborn, surely? No, that's not a condition. And be free, no slaves allowed surely? No, that's not a condition. And be just male, or female, or straight, or gay, or sick, or well, or old, or young or whatever restrictions you try to include? No, that's not a condition.

You see, God doesn't save you because you are specially good or holy. Quite the opposite. Salvation isn't rooted in what you are like, but what God is like. And God says today that whoever you are, whatever you are, wherever you come from, 'If you declare with your mouth that "Jesus is Lord," and believe in your heart that God raised him from the dead, you will be saved… for everybody who calls on the name of the

18

# BELIEVE!

Lord will be saved.' Which of course, includes you. Believe it, receive it, and live it. Amen.

# 2

# GOD KNOWS

I've preached this sermon a number of times and in slightly variant forms. It seeks to engage with a common issue for Christians – God's guidance. It first arose during a time when I was myself seeking guidance for a particular decision in life and, consequently, like many of my sermons, is preached to myself as well as those I am preaching to. All preachers tend to preach sermons they themselves need!

Readings: Jeremiah 29:4-14 & John 14:1-7.

As a family of Christian people we gather in different circumstances. Some of us are extremely positive about the future, some are in fear or even dread; some of us are full of plans and some completely at a loss. So I want to preach from that famous verse in Jeremiah 29:11, '*I know the plans I have for you, plans for good and not for evil, to give you a future and a hope*,' and particularly the first eight words – I know – the plans – I have – for you.

### '*I know* the plans…'
In the twelve years I was at Cliff College I spent lots of time with students who were trying to discern the will of God. Some would sit on the couch, often anxious and serious, and say something like this: 'I wish I knew what God is calling me into. I'd love God to tell me if I'm going to get married, especially if it's while I'm here,

and how many children I will have, and if will I be happy. Will I be called abroad? Will I have enough money to live? Will I become a famous preacher, and I wonder when I will die… you see, I just want to live by faith!' I hope you note the irony!

I reminded them – as I remind us all this morning – that as disciples of Jesus we are called to walk by faith and not by sight. I reminded them that to entrust yourself to God and live faithfully while not knowing how it's all going to turn out marks a deeper kind of trust and faith than having everything mapped out. I reminded them too that for the disciples of Christ, in the end, it's more important that God knows the plans than that they do. And I told them that the worst of all worlds was that they had lots of plans that God knew nothing about!

'*I know the plans,*' God says. You might not, fully, yet. Indeed we may never fully know God's plans for us. But I want you to know and believe that the fact that God knows the plans is more important than that we know the plans. For the disciples, that's enough, and I urge us all to live as if that's enough.

## 'I know *the plans…*'

It is 'plans' – plural, not a 'plan' – singular. There's not one static, defined, unalterable plan. God doesn't have 'a plan' in the sense that if I miss that single moment, turn left instead of right, or choose wrongly in August 1993, then I've blown it for ever: no reprieve, no second chance. This is important to note, because I know some people who sadly live as if that was exactly what the plan of their life is like. They feel they messed it up and are now just treading water, endlessly regretting whatever they thought was God's plan for them before they blew it. It's important because I also know church congregations who live and act as if all God had planned for them was somehow used up long ago, and they now have little sense of purpose. But there are plan*s*.

I remember the first time I ever came across GPS, the Sat Nav, many years ago now. It was in a luxury car belonging to my friend

Neil, and I was mesmerised by the moving map and the silky voice of a famous actress speaking the instructions. Neil proudly showed it off. We approached a junction and our GPS guide said, 'In two hundred yards, turn left.' It was at this point that we demonstrated that sin still has firm hold on us! A glint came into my eye and I said to Neil, 'What happens if you don't do as she says?' A glint came into his eye and he said, 'Watch this.' We approached the next junction and the GPS voice said, 'Turn right'… and we went straight on.

The voice was quiet for a few moments then revealed that this GPS was both Christian and Wesleyan! Because the Sat Nav said these gospel words… 'I have worked out a new route for you.'

*Waterfalls in Guangdong province, China. H. Atkins*

There is only one right destination, to be where God wants you, in God's will and way. But this means that when we go wrong, or go cold, or become disobedient and lose the plot – and some of us do and some of us will – God, the redeeming, forgiving, wonderful One works out a new route, and wills us to follow it. There are plans.

This is not an excuse to be lax in our discipleship. It's not an encouragement to become like those who walk into sinful ways, eyes wide open, then shrug their shoulders and say, 'God will forgive me, it's God's business to.' It's a word of hope and grace to those of us who struggle, and fail, but desire and resolve to continue the long journey of following Jesus.

Some of us have blown it many times. To you, I say remember, God has plans – plural – for you. And even when you believed that a plan was perfect, and understood it as God's will, then it fell apart – the job crumbles, the relationship dissolves, whatever – then I gently say to you today that was the end of that plan, but not the end of all the plans, the possible plans, that God has for you.

### 'I know the plans *I have for you*'

Do you remember the students at Cliff College sitting on the couch talking about discerning God's guidance I mentioned earlier? Some of them even thought I was wise! After I'd encouraged them to live by faith and not by sight, and trust in God for the way ahead, they would sigh and say, 'I don't know what God wants of me.' And I would reply, 'Oh, I do,' and they would lean forward with interest, all ears. 'Please tell me,' they'd say. So I did.

'God wants you to become more like Christ,' I'd tell them. 'God wants you to permit your life in all its aspects to become ever more filled with the Holy Spirit so that there's no room for anything else. God wants you to pray and seek his face. God wants you to live in peace with all, as much as it lies with you. God wants you to love your neighbour as yourself. God wants you to have a sober judgment about yourself. God wants you to realise that if you hold on to your life you will lose it, but if you lose your life for Christ's sake and the sake of the gospel, you will never lose it. God wants you to become what God yearns for you to become. I know this is God's plan for you because it's God's plan for all of us, every one of us.'

Some students understood, and some didn't. The ones that didn't looked disappointed and said, 'Yes, I know all that, but I thought you were going to tell me the plans God has for ME.'

I'd reply something like this. 'In the wonder of God's grace there is a unique 'you.' It may be that God has plans for you and you alone, specific plans that are peculiarly yours in addition to the marvellous plans God has for us all, plans that have your fingerprint attached.' And not wishing to lose my reputation as a wise one I would add, 'I don't know exactly what special plans

God has for you, but I do know the best way to find out what they might be.'

And again they would lean forward on the couch, all ears. 'Please,' they'd say, 'tell me.' And I said to them what I say to you and to me – for I too know what it is to seek the guidance of God: 'Be faithful to all that God wants and plans for us all, and you will discover what God plans for you and you alone. Seek first the kingdom of God and everything else will be added to you. Do all the other stuff seriously and thoroughly. And that special stuff will be added to you. Ignore all the other stuff and you lessen your chances of ever coming to know or appreciate those specific plans God may have for you.'

I became aware this past week of one of the plans God has for us all. I went to visit a long-time friend, a minister in Christ's Church, who was fit and healthy just a month ago and is now having hospice care at home, terminally ill. Bless him, among all the symptoms of irreversible illness there was a live faith. He said croakily – his voice is affected, a poignant thing for a preacher – 'I am going to be with the Lord. I will see his face. I am going to live with him forever.' You see, any plans he may have had from this time forward must now fall – the time for them has gone. And as I drove home I realised how we will all reach that time one day. There is deep sadness, leaving those you love, wrestling with the timing and the raw fact of it all. But there is also the promise of life with God forever. God knows the plans in life, and God knows the plans after our physical death. And they are wonderful.

So, if you're away from or outside of God's plans and you know it – come back! If you've got plans that God knows nothing about – ditch them! If you're dubious about God's plans – remember God knows best! If you're wanting to know God's special plans for you – get all the wonderfully ordinary stuff of Christian discipleship sorted – it's the best way to know the special stuff. And know too that just as God has plans for our lives, God has plans for our eternal lives. So let's live – and in time die – knowing and believing that God knows, and that, ultimately, at the end of everything, that's alright with us. Amen.

# 3

# COMMON CLAY POTS

There's an established and well regarded Christian healing ministry at MCHW. Monthly healing services take place in the evening and a few morning services a year are given over to 'healing' themes. This sermon was preached sat down, on my return from several weeks' convalescence following ankle surgery and while still using crutches. It included a response, inviting people to come and take a piece of broken pottery as a symbol of identity and commitment. The strand of comic irony and allusive language running through the sermon is deliberate!

Readings: 2 Corinthians 4:5-11 & John 6:35-37.

*'But we have this treasure in clay pots, so that it may be made clear that this extraordinary power belongs to God and does not come from us.'*

I want to talk a little about common clay pots.

In spite of all the environmental damage they do it's hardly surprising that plastic bottles, bin bags, and tin cans are so much more popular today than clay. Clay. What stuff! It weighs a ton and is just so breakable, so fragile. It cracks so easily. I remember that nice clay pot I bought in Africa as a gift. I wrapped it up so carefully and took great care with my bag, but it was still in pieces by the time I got home. Clay? Hopeless stuff!

But you see, God loves common clay pots. It's not that God discriminates against cola cans or plastic bottles, you understand, but God made the clay. Oh, I know God made everything, but he made the clay, at the beginning of time, when the world was new. At one time it was just dirt. But God spat into the dirt and like a potter made something of the clay, and out of it came… humans. Remember Genesis? How God breathed life into the clay so that it ceased to be an 'it' and became a living soul. Remember? How God sits back on the sixth day and looks at what he's made and says, 'That's good.'

Our eldest son did pottery at school and ceramics at university and now works in a university ceramics department. He can make much nicer things now than he first did, but do you think we threw his early efforts away? What you make first is always special, always precious. So in the beginning, God made human clay pots, and I guess that's why God loves them so much.

*Cracked pot. B. Atkins*

Not only that. God loves *cracked* and *broken* common clay pots! We tend to forget that as he writes this passage Paul is suffering – probably physically, mentally and emotionally. He's going to go on to talk about a thorn in the flesh, a dogged condition – some have suggested he had epilepsy, others that he had a hunched back that's not been rectified in spite of fervent prayer. '*Three times I sought the Lord,*' he writes, '*and he said to me, "My grace is sufficient for you."*' More painful still, some are saying that because of Paul's suffering, because of what he looks like, he is ungodly, and his ministry is to be rejected. 'How,' they say, 'can God use a person who is so weak, fragile and looks like this?'

28

# COMMON CLAY POTS

But you see our sufferings aren't automatically connected to sin or faithlessness. Though that's what opponents of Paul were saying. In one sense, our times of suffering are the means of our renewal and growth in discipleship. Discipleship of Christ takes place and deepens in common cracked clay pots. Weakness, fragility, suffering and disability don't mean that a person is not anointed, or their ministry marred. Think for a moment! Our ministry is derived from and inspired by a suffering Lord Jesus.

Discipleship is not about having no pain, no deprivation, no health conditions or no fragilities. No. It's how you deal with these things that matters. Martin Niemöller, in a concentration camp in World War Two said, 'I cannot stop what is being done to me, but the one thing that nobody can take away from me is my choice about how I respond to what is being done to me.'

Now we know about God's healing power, and we believe in it. But we need to be careful about the teaching of healing that moves us into what might be called the 'perfectionist' mode. It moves us to believe a world portrayed by TV adverts where smiles are permanent and perfect, bodies are all blemish-free and marvellous, because of course God wants us all to be perfect – like supermodels! That's what healing is, isn't it?

Today let's listen to a deeper, more wonderful gospel truth. The treasure of Christ is found in common cracked clay pots – like you and like me. We come together here with our addictions, conditions, terminal diseases, and breakdowns. We're on crutches, in wheelchairs, and propped up with all sorts of things that you can't see on the outside. At one level we look more broken and frail, fragile and pathetic when such folk are in our midst. But at a deeper level we are more whole, more complete. You see, it's not until we are the company of the healthy and the physically and mentally cracked and broken ones that we are truly the body of Christ. Because his body is a broken body. It has spear marks and thorns and splinters. It has the signs of mental agony and anxiety. Because even in resurrection glory, Jesus is known by the scars.

A woman had undergone surgery for a lump in her mouth. She was recovering after surgery, her husband was with her, and the surgeon came to visit. He said to the woman, 'I'm sorry to say that the lump we've removed was cancerous. I'm confident that we've got it all and taken it away. But you will need more treatment and it's likely your mouth will be partly paralysed and a little disfigured all your life.' The husband puts his arm round his wife as the news sinks in, and the surgeon says he'll be back and makes for the door. But as he turns he sees the husband lean over and very gently kiss his wife, and notices that he shapes his lips to fit her new misshapenness.

Now that is what God in Christ does. He takes our shape. Our mis-shape. And he kisses life and love into twisted, frail, broken people. We're not made perfect like supermodels. But we are made new. A treasure in common clay pots. So this is the place of the fragile, cracked, broken, clay pot people. And if that includes you, you are welcome here, and you're acceptable to God. Because God loves common cracked clay pots. *'We have this treasure,'* says Paul, *'in clay pots, so that it may be made clear that this extraordinary power belongs to God and does not come from us.'* Some of us need to hear that today.

So, God loves common clay pots. God loves common, cracked clay pots. And, lastly, cracked and broken clay pots are often the kind that serve Christ and bear witness to Christ best of all!

I was talking to a Methodist local preacher who has multiple sclerosis. She said, 'When I was well I got the impression that nobody really listened to me. Now, I arrive in my chair and preach about God's love, and they hang on every word.' You see, cracked clay pots can't keep the treasure inside. It leaks out, through the cracks. It's possible for complete, sealed clay pots to contain that treasure, and for nobody to know it's there. But that's not possible for cracked clay pots. It just has to come out.

Some aspects of renewal are a bit like trying to take a drink from a firehose – you get a lot on you but not much in you! But being a cracked clay pot is about the drip, drip, drip, of precious treasure going in, and the constant drip, drip, drip, as it leaks out. Us, little us, creaking, cracked, frail, filled with God's gospel treasure and therefore somehow wonderfully complete and whole.

Look at the couplets Paul uses in the passage. We are afflicted but not crushed, perplexed but not driven to despair, persecuted but not forsaken, struck down but not destroyed. Paul is cracked, but not cracked up. He is a cracked pot, but not a crackpot!

The point of this list is not that we admire the unquenchability of the human spirit under adversity, but that we give all credit to God who is able to sustain through every circumstance. Couplets were a traditional Hellenist rhetorical device whereby speakers outlined trials to be undergone and urged the need for stoic courage and fortitude as they were faced. By contrast, Paul uses this rhetoric device with a different application – the glory of God. Paul's hardships proclaim the power of God in human weakness.

Make no mistake, the most effective witnesses and evangelists of Christ today – and tomorrow – are not well dressed, smooth-talking, ever-smiling perfectionists of yesteryear. They are 2 Corinthians 4 people. Common cracked clay pot people who embody the frailty, the cost and the glory of Christian discipleship.

And as we listen to Paul's words, perhaps we catch a glimpse of another image. Of a suffering servant. Because the passion and dying and rising and resurrection of Jesus rings through this passage like a bell. God's divine presence is evident in the frailty of Jesus, in the frailty of Paul, and in your own frailty. That is our hope.

In excavations in caves in the Middle East some clay pots were discovered dating back to near the time of Christ. Some were intact and sealed, some were cracked, and some smashed and broken. They opened a couple of the sealed clay pots and found inside scented ointment, preserved just as it was almost two millennia ago. They carefully removed all the intact pots but noticed that the smell of the precious ointment remained. On investigation, they discovered the smell came from the shards of broken pots. After many hundreds of years, with no visible sign of the scented ointment left, the fragrance remained. The fragrance was not in the pot, it was the pot. The broken pot and the fragrance had become one.

For those who want to respond in some way, here are baskets of broken clay pots. As we sing, you may want to come and pick a piece. You don't have to say anything, but some of you tell me you are helped by suggestions of what might be said at such times as these. I will be saying something like this. 'I'm broken, Lord. But I am yours.' And if you listen very carefully you might hear Jesus speak to you. 'I am broken too. And I am yours.' Amen.

# 4

# NON PLUS ULTRA?

The first time I ever heard this phrase, I was listening to Dr. William Davies (past Principal of Cliff College and President of the Methodist Conference) preach. It was very many years ago and I don't think I've 'borrowed' much from his sermon save the theme inherent in the phrase itself. But if I have I'm sure Bill is fine with that! This sermon was preached on the first Sunday of a new Methodist year, which begins in September. There is not the dedicatory intensity of, say, a Methodist covenant service. But nevertheless, as summer ends and schools begin again, there's always a sense of a starting point, which can of course be regarded as a repetitive grind or a new, exciting beginning.

Readings: Philippians 3:4-16 & John 6:67-69.

'In fourteen hundred and ninety two'... what's next? ('Columbus sailed the ocean blue'.) Before that time, maps had written on them at various points the Latin phrase '*ne – or non – plus ultra*' – meaning there's 'nothing more beyond.' Similarly, the Pillars of Hercules, two promontories marking out the Strait of Gibraltar, the then edge of the classical ancient world, had inscribed on them *non plus ultra*. Declaring, in effect, to sailors and explorers as they set sail, 'This is the end of the world.' And remember, the world was still thought to be flat and, therefore, you could fall off it! So go no further. *Non plus ultra* – there's nothing more beyond.

# NEW WESTMINSTER SERMONS

The phrase *non plus ultra* was found not only on maps and ancient pillars, but also on coins. When Christopher Columbus was small, in the 1470s, some Spanish and Portuguese coins had on them *Ne plus ultra*, a proud boast by the two leading rulers of the seas and explorers of the world at that time, that there was nothing more beyond where we have gone, nothing else to find. Wrongly as it turned out. Because in 1492 Columbus, we are told, discovered the New World. And by the time he died, in 1506, both Spanish and Portuguese coins had on them *plus ultra* – there is something more, something beyond. So today, if you visit Columbus' memorial in Valladolid in Spain, you'll see that the first word of the phrase *non plus ultra* is being eaten by a lion, leaving *plus ultra*.

Today marks another new Methodist church year, and I want to use the occasion to ask each of us how we approach it. Do we enter this new year with a *plus ultra* spirit? Are we full of expectation and excitement about what more God is going to do in us, and with us and through us? Or do we have a *non plus ultra* mentality? Expecting nothing much, nothing more, in terms of the height, length and breadth of God.

Let me list some symptoms of a *non plus ultra* mentality. Has complacency with the Christian story set in? Have we become closed to being taught new things? Do we hear Scripture read and say, 'I know this one,' and not listen further? Do we sit through sermons assuming nothing will become the loud, fresh, necessary word of God for us? Do we sing 'Love divine, all loves excelling,' on automatic pilot, unconscious of what we're saying? Do we approach the Lord's table thinking, 'Boring, it's just bread and wine again'?

Do we look at the many ministries and groups in the church starting up for another year, and groan? Do we say, 'I'll not bother enlisting on the discipleship course, attending the prayer meeting, or Bible study, or house group. I don't think I'll join the flower team, or the communion team, or the counting team, or the refreshments team, the bookstall team, the welcome team or the information desk team. I can't offer to go on the crèche rota, or help lead Sunday school, or the Young People's Fellowship… I'm going to decline the request for helpers with our 'Welcome to refugees' ministry and the winter night shelter for the homeless. I don't think I will increase my giving, or donate more regularly to the foodbank, or offer to become a steward.' And this is not to mention the wide world of noble and good causes outside the life of the church that are crying out for followers of Christ to join and partner.

Now I say all this not to guilt-trip you! Nor to shame you into doing something that's not right for you to do. God knows our circumstances. I say this to describe the *non plus ultra* syndrome. A spiritual mindset that there's nothing more. That my Christian life of discipleship is stuck. And worst of all, if I'm being honest, that I'm content it is so. Or maybe not?

The early disciples of Jesus must have been tempted to move into *non plus ultra* mode – at times when they thought, 'There's nothing more than this.' There they are, listening to the Sermon on the Mount and thinking, 'What an amazing teacher, surely there's nothing better and beyond this?' There they are, watching as Jesus gives sight to a blind man, cures a leper, and raises Lazarus from the dead, and they are gobsmacked each time. 'What an amazing healer, surely there's nothing better and beyond this?' There they are, in the garden as he is arrested. Horrified, as he is tried and beaten up and sentenced. Mortified as he is crucified. This is the end, they think. *Non plus ultra*. There's nothing more. So that when women come and tell them he's alive, at first they don't and can't believe it. And then… he's there. With them. Alive. Again. Amazing! Surely there's nothing beyond this?

Then, before they get used to having him with them again, he's gone! They're told to wait for power from on high, but it's frightened, un-bold, unready disciples who are in a closed room in Jerusalem on the day of Pentecost. They think they've received all that Jesus gave them and they don't think it's enough. And the Holy Spirit falls upon them and they're never the same again. Now they understand better what Jesus meant when he said, 'Go, be my disciples, and make disciples, and I will be with you forever.'

When did you move into the *non plus ultra* mode? At the teaching? At the healings? At the suffering? At the cross? At the resurrection? So many of us never get to Pentecost. At some point of the story we decide there's nothing more – or we want nothing more, seek nothing more. *Non plus ultra*.

But hear this please. Disciples who think they have all that Jesus wants to give them discover there is something more. Because we are a *plus ultra* people of a *plus ultra* God! And I urge you to devote time and prayer and effort in working out what the *plus ultra* of discipleship is, for you, this new Methodist year!

Now I do recognise that our ability to receive this message today is determined in significant part by our circumstances. If we're struggling with illness, or pain, or old age, or dealing with depression, or anxiety, or bereavement, the urge to something more is received differently to those of us who are feeling that God is calling us into new things, and that we're up for it. To that person this is a sermon of confirmation and encouragement. To others, this is a sermon that possibly frustrates or even angers.

I'm mindful that it was at this equivalent service, almost two years ago to the day, that I came out of this pulpit to discover my father had died while I preached. I'm not alone in that experience of bereavement. Far from it. All of us know the loss of loved ones. So I remind myself and I remind you that ours is a *plus ultra* faith, not merely to urge us to greater action or service, but to grasp afresh that our faith is that even death is not the end. There is something beyond. Made possible by the life and death and resurrection of Jesus. It's the promise of heaven and eternal life. It's this promise, this gift, this assurance, that enables us to enter a new year of life and discipleship saying that whatever our circumstances – there is something more, something beyond. So take heart and take faith!

Some of you will have come across the phrase *non –* or *ne – plus ultra* before, and some won't. If you go home and look it up online you might think I've been spinning you a yarn all morning. Because nowadays *non plus ultra* is often used differently to how I've been applying it. Today, it's used to indicate perfection; there is nothing else needed or beyond this. It is the peak, the summit, the zenith, the pinnacle, the crown, the ultimate.

*Something beyond. H. Atkins*

This is the one and only way in which *non plus ultra*, rather than *plus ultra* applies to Christianity. For beyond Christ there is nothing. He is the image of the invisible God in whom all the fullness of God was pleased to dwell. He is the Way, the Truth and the Life. He is the perfect humanity on which to model our own lives.

The disciples came to recognise this. It was a new season of following him – a bit like a new church year beginning – and many were walking away from following him. Jesus asked the disciples, 'Will you give up? Have you had enough? Is it for you *non plus ultra*?' 'Lord,' they reply, 'where else would we go, you have the words of eternal life.' They came to know what I urge us to hold to again today, there is no one like him or beyond him. Jesus Christ is the true *non plus ultra*, so that we can be *plus ultra* people. Whatever our circumstances today, let's resolve anew and afresh to be so. Amen.

# 5

# 'ALL THIS FOR YOU'

**Preached at a service in which the infant granddaughter of my colleague Revd Tony Miles had been baptised. Tony proudly administered baptism, clearly moved as he addressed Sienna, using the words in the Methodist Worship Book which rehearse the life, death and resurrection of Christ, and saying directly to the uncomprehending infant, 'All this for you'. It was the Sunday after Christmas. Sienna's parents, Tony's daughter and son-in-law, who live abroad, were visiting. Christians themselves, they'd invited lots of friends to be present, many of whom weren't Christians or regular churchgoers, and urged me to 'preach the gospel' in this context.**

I want to speak about the baptism we've participated in earlier in this service, and in doing so remind us that it's Christmas!

When a group of us were first writing the services in the Methodist Worship Book – and I had the privilege of sharing in the writing of them – I remember the time we wrote the baptism services, one of which we used today for Sienna's baptism. We had one hilarious day in a conference centre when we went through each baptism service, complete with an old teddy bear as the baby, who was wet through by the time we'd finished trying out all the services. How much better having a real, live baby here this morning!

I remember too when we first came across a version of the words which, amended a little, are used in the baptismal service;

words I find so moving still, each time they're used. Words that are particularly poignant at Christmas time, when we celebrate Jesus Christ, God with us, God made human, coming as a baby, born of Mary. Tony said: 'Sienna, for you Jesus Christ came into the world, for you he lived and showed God's love; for you he suffered death on the Cross, for you he triumphed over death rising to newness of life; for you he prays at God's right hand. *All this for you*, before you could know anything of it…'

And he said all this to Sienna! It's tempting to say that's just silly. I mean, why bother when she can't understand you? But of course we all talk to babies before they can understand what's being said. That's how they learn to speak. And if we only said things to people when we were sure they'd understand them, we'd barely say anything to anyone! But also we speak these words because they're true. And that's rather wonderful!

One of the most important things any person can do is choose to follow Jesus Christ. To come to regard Jesus not simply a person in history but to know him as a living Lord and leader of our lives. I first decided to follow Jesus Christ in a nightclub in the early hours of the morning. Another story for another time! When I chose to become a Christian, I didn't understand everything, but I understood enough to begin to believe that Jesus was God's special one, that he came to rescue me from the worst versions of me, and be there with me as I sought to live my life in the best way possible. I consciously said to Christ what millions of people have said down the centuries: 'If you are real Lord, be real to me.'

From that day, many years ago, in lots of significant and almost imperceptible ways, Jesus became real, and became – to use religious language – my Lord and my Saviour. To all those who have never taken that leap of faith, I commend Jesus to you. Christians refer to the life and words of Jesus as the gospel, which means good news. Because it is good news that God loves us, good news that through Jesus our sins are forgiven, good news that God wants to share our lives, lead us wisely and finally take us to heaven. Some of us here will want – even need – to hear the good news of love, and forgiveness, and acceptance and promise. Jesus, the baby of Bethlehem and the one who died on the cross, offers that good news to you and me.

When I became a Christian all those years ago, and people asked me to explain it – a bit like I have just now – I used words like 'I believe Jesus has died for me,' 'I believe God loves me.' Now, here's the thing. These things are true. But they didn't become true because I came to believe it. They *were* true and I came to realise they were true. Jesus Christ loves me whether I love him or not. Jesus Christ died on the cross for my sins, to set me free, whether I accept that or not. You see, the gospel of Jesus is always on offer before demand, so that the demand is always made possible by the offer.

That's why, in the baptism service of a baby like Sienna, we declare what's true before she knows it, but pray and work hard so that what we have declared to be true comes true in her life. That's one reason why Sienna's parents only made promises of their own about Sienna *after* she was baptised, not before. We don't declare the promises of God over Sienna because *we* make promises: we make promises because what God has done for us is true. We love, because God in Christ first loved us.

At Christmastime we see that demonstrated again. God doesn't come to us in the baby Jesus because we deserve it, but because we don't. Jesus doesn't come to us as a reward but as a promise. But there is demand on us all, as we respond to God's love. The demand on parents at the baptism of their child is to be good parents, to love and care for their child, to raise them well. The demand on friends of the family in a baptism service is to offer love, and friendship, and support to them in raising their children well. The demand on us all is to respond positively to God's love and invitation to follow Christ.

About Christianity some parents say, 'I'll let my child decide. I don't want to brainwash her.'

I understand that – I don't approve of brainwashing either. But then we don't leave our children hungry, or wet, or dirty, or uneducated, saying, 'I'll let them decide.' So here in baptism we all signal our dedication to the good task.

Some say your baptism doesn't matter because you can't remember it! But all sorts of crucial things happen and we can't remember them! Our birth for example. Or what happens during an operation under general anaesthetic! Just because we don't remember something, it doesn't mean it didn't happen, or that it didn't do what it was intended to do.

So when we baptise someone in Jesus name, however young or old they are, when promises are made, when – whether years from now, or today – we make a choice to follow Jesus, to make him our Lord, there is rejoicing in heaven, there is blessing. Because before ever we come to know and love him – he loves us. Known and loved. Loved and known. Amazing love! Praise God! Amen.

# 6

# GRACE UPON GRACE

The first of three Wesley or Aldersgate Sunday sermons and therefore with an explicit Methodist and Wesleyan content, while being aware that, as in most congregations of any size in this post-denominational age, not all hearers will be Methodists or know much about John or Charles Wesley. The 'turtle' story or application is borrowed, if I recall correctly, from Dr. George (Chuck) Hunter III, who was a significant source of encouragement when I started teaching adults.

**Reading: Philippians 2:5-13.**

It's Aldersgate Sunday, which will mean something to some of us and not much to others. It's the occasion when Methodist Christians remember their earthly origins and particularly the ministry of the key founders of Methodism, John and Charles Wesley. Brothers. Anglican clergymen. One a superb hymn-writer and speaker; the other a brilliant organiser and networker. Quite different in temperament but both used mightily of God during much of the 18th century. Together with increasing numbers of others they led and coordinated the fastest growing Christian movement in modern British history: what became the Methodist Church now has some seventy-five million members throughout the world.

It's said of Methodists today that they fall into two groups in relation to the Wesleys. The first group doesn't know they lived and the second group doesn't know they've died! I want to walk a middle way this morning. It's right that we know a little about them, but without suggesting that their every hymn, word, book and sermon decisively determines our discipleship today. Because they had some wacky ideas. John Wesley published a book called *Primitive Physick* in which, among many novel remedies for all sorts of common ailments was the suggestion that the cure for baldness was rubbing raw onion into the scalp!

We're on much sounder ground looking at the faith that fired John and Charles, what they passionately believed about God. So today, in what is mainly a teaching sermon I want to talk about God's grace.

A professor of philosophy was with her class. Each student was asked to state their understanding of life, the universe and everything. One student said, 'Life is a giant turtle!' 'Okay,' said the professor, 'but what's under the turtle?' 'Another turtle,' said the student. 'But what's under that turtle?' persisted the professor. 'Look prof,' said the student, 'let's cut to the chase. It's turtles all the way down!'

When John and Charles Wesley talked about the nature of God – Father, Son and Holy Spirit – they said, in effect, 'It's simple and it's wonderful. It's grace – all the way down!' They talked about God's grace in relation to human life in three overlapping ways, and I want to outline these.

First, they taught about God's prevenient grace. 'Pre' meaning 'before', 'venient' meaning 'coming' – so 'grace that comes before.' Before what? Before any conscious experience of divine saving grace and awareness of God. But we must start further back, like the turtles. Because prevenient grace arose from a piece of theological logic. It goes like this. The Bible teaches that all people are born in sin. We are members of a sinful race. We aren't sinners because we commit sin. We commit sin because we're sinners. Sin doesn't attach itself to humans like barnacles on a ship. It doesn't sneak up on you; it arises out of you. Sin, then, is a sickness which makes us sick to death. And we're unable by our own efforts to make the slightest move towards God.

Yet God offers salvation to all, and that offer must be real because God isn't going to offer something impossible to be received. That would be cruel and God is anything but cruel. So, it must be possible to accept God's offer of salvation. But how? How is our inability to respond to God because of our paralysing sinfulness and God's offer of salvation to be reconciled?

It's in this context that Methodists talk about God's *prevenient* grace. We might experience our first, weakest wish to please God, a moment of briefest illumination about God's will and nature, our initial awareness that we are not, in relation to God, what we should be or desire to be. Such things are 'evidence' of God's prevenient grace. To be sure, not everyone would recognise them as such, and humans can reject or deny them. But before ever we knew of it God was moving, calling, inviting, going before in our lives. We see this poetically and beautifully in the Methodist baptism service, when we say to the baby – not its parents – 'For you Jesus Christ came into the world. For you he lived and died, for you he was raised from death. All this for you. Before you could know anything of it.'

But prevenient grace wasn't sufficient, of itself, to bring about justification and faith. So the Wesleys also talked and taught of *justifying* grace. *Saving* grace. Saved from our sins by the grace of God through the work of Christ, God's Son. The Wesleys understood this grace as being free *in* all and free *for* all. God's grace is free and it's universal, offered to all people. Which meant there's not one person on this planet, and never has been, for whom God's grace has not been offered. Because, God in Jesus Christ died, once for all.

This doesn't mean that everyone will be saved, but it does mean that everyone can be saved. When people asked, 'How is it some people are saved and some are not?' the Wesleys pointed out our free choice to choose faith or reject it. To those who claimed,

'We can do absolutely nothing in relation to our salvation,' John Wesley said, to innumerable crowds, 'You can choose Christ.'

So saving faith is offered as God's free grace gift, but each person must choose whether or not to receive the gift, to open the present. This is what Charles Wesley was getting at when he wrote: *He left his Father's throne above – so free, so infinite his grace – emptied himself of all but love, and bled for Adam's helpless race... Long my imprisoned spirit lay fast bound in sin and nature's night; thine eye diffused a quickening ray. I woke, the dungeon flamed with light, my chains fell off, my heart was free, I rose, went forth, and followed thee.*

The Wesleys also sang and spoke about *sanctifying* grace. If salvation comes about sometimes in an instant and sometimes more gradually, then sanctification is, by definition, a gradual affair. 'From grace to grace,' as the Wesleys put it. Sanctification requires continuing repentance and growth in grace and good works, and the evidence of being sanctified is continuing faith responses to God's gracious initiatives. Because grace can be resisted at any point in time, at which point sanctification stalls. The Wesleys didn't teach 'permanent perfection' – once attained, always attained. A person could fall from perfection at any time, but could also attain it at any time. But they also taught that the divine grace that sanctified a person also sustained them and so God provided everything necessary to aid our growth in faith and holiness.

Methodists referred to this process as 'perfect – or perfecting – love,' 'entire sanctification,' and 'holiness.' Holiness was understood supremely about becoming more like the Holy One, Jesus. Jesus, who showed us how to live, and die, what was worth living for, and who calls us to live for him. That's what the powerful passage from Philippians we read today is all about. To quote Charles Wesley again: '*Changed from glory into glory, till in heaven we take our place, till we cast our crowns before thee, lost in wonder, love, and praise!*'

So perhaps we see how grace – like the turtles – goes all the way down. Grace is God's very nature. Grace upon grace.

I want us to note a few brief things, because they're wonderful and hope-giving.

First, the Wesleys taught and believed and practised the

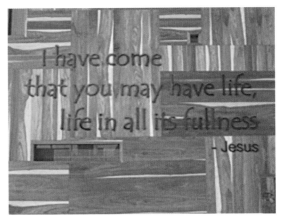

*Doors at Seth Mokitimi Seminary, S A. M. Atkins*

grace of God that is active in every phase of human life. There's not a point in our lives when God's grace isn't active in us and with us. During depression? Yes. Despair? Yes. Valleys of the shadow of death? Yes. Prevenient grace woos us, saving grace saves us from our sins, sanctifying and sustaining grace meets us at our points of need and equips us with courage and strength. Grace doesn't mean the absence of struggle, but it promises the presence of God. Grace, you see, is more than we deserve and greater than we imagine. And grace is the very nature of the one who says to us, 'I will never leave you or forsake you.'

Second, grace is grace. I've divided up the applications of grace for the sake of clarity. But in fact there isn't one kind of grace for one situation and another sort of grace for another. God doesn't give grace in bits and pieces. We experience God's grace differently in different situations, and grace comes to us at different points of our journey, and it has different effects on us, and it evokes different responses in us. But it's all grace. And it is the very nature of God.

Third, the Wesleys used the term 'grace' in two ways, almost automatically. Grace is the undeserved favour and freely given love of God, and it's also the active power and help of God. Grace is the voice of God that both tells us to change and offers the power to pull it off. God doesn't wait for us to become clean; God comes and offers to clean us up. Because when we give ourselves to Christ, he gives himself to us, having given himself for us. Then all things become possible.

Fourth, grace goes beyond mercy. It goes all the way down. Mercy gave the prodigal son a second chance; grace throws him a party. Mercy prompts the Samaritan to bandage the wounds of the victim; grace has him leave his credit card to pay for the victim's care. Mercy forgave the thief on the cross; grace escorted him into paradise. Mercy pardons us; grace loves us.

The big question for us all today is how we respond to a God of grace? God who never gives up on us and who never leaves us without the ability to change. God who goes beyond what we deserve. Who saves us, and saves us completely, in Jesus our Lord.

The Wesleys' response to that question was to urge us humbly and repeatedly to say 'Yes' to God in Christ. I hope you will say 'Yes' to One like that, even now? One way to say 'Yes' is to sing the next hymn from the heart: *Son of God; if your free grace again has raised me up, called me still to seek your face, and given me back my hope; still your timely help afford, and all your loving-kindness show: keep me, keep me, gracious Lord, and never let me go!* Amen.

# 7

# BE BEING FILLED

Preached in the week leading up to Halloween, though not technically a Halloween or All Saints Day sermon.

Readings: Acts 10:44-48 & Luke 11:9-13.

From the earliest times it has been clear that to be a Christian, a disciple, a follower of Jesus, is to be filled with the Holy Spirit of God. Time after time in the Acts of the Apostles the Holy Spirit falls upon those who desire Christ, and very often in relation to being baptised, as we saw in our reading from Acts 10. In fact, so normal is the expectation that believers in Christ will be filled with the Spirit that when it doesn't happen, it's unusual. So when Paul comes across some believers in Ephesus, in Acts 19, he asks them, 'Were you baptised with the Holy Spirit when you believed?' 'No, we haven't even heard that there is a Holy Spirit,' they reply. On hearing this, Paul baptises them in the name of Jesus Christ, lays his hands upon them, and they are filled with the Holy Spirit. And when, years later, Paul writes to the Christian believers in Ephesus, he tells them, 'Be filled with the Spirit.'

I became a Christian in the 1970s, and my early Christian life was shaped by what we then called the charismatic renewal. The charismatic renewal didn't get everything right. But it did get at least one thing very right. It reminded mainline Christianity that it had often become Holy Spirit 'lite', a Christian faith that focused on the nature of God the Father and Jesus the Son, but comparatively little on the Holy Spirit. The charismatic renewal urged us to regard 'normal' Christianity – rather than 'abnormal' Christianity – as Christian faith, filled and fuelled, emboldened and enabled, strengthened and sustained by the Holy Spirit of God.

Today I want to talk about being filled with God's Holy Spirit – about 'normal' Christian life.

I want to start with a negative question, simply because in my experience it's where many of us actually begin. It's this: 'Why are we not filled with the Holy Spirit?' One key reason why many of us aren't filled with the Holy Spirit is because we're full of stuff already. Junk mainly. Like my loft at home. Like the back room in my office at work. It's already stuffed full – and mostly with things I don't really need. To ask God to fill us with the Holy Spirit would likely result in the same response I give anyone wanting to put more stuff in my back office: 'You're going to have to get rid of some stuff before you can put anything more in there.'

The early Christians recognised this reality as common in human beings. In the ancient catechesis – meaning 'teaching,' usually prior to being baptised – you were asked to examine each bit of your life – your practices, morals, relationships and so on – and everything that was not of God was removed by prayer and the laying on of hands. Things were 'taken out of you,' and sometimes even 'pulled out' of lives full of junk, stuff that prevented there being space for God's Spirit to enter and fill. It's hardly surprising, is it? An adult human is full of all sorts of junk accumulated over years of this and that, this practice and that sin, this habit and that experience. And into these newly cleared spaces the catechists – teachers – prayed that the Holy Spirit would come, and fill the space. Else they be like the woman in the gospels who's delivered of one bad thing only to be filled with several more. So, gradually, bit by bit, these trainee disciples, undergoing training for the baptism that would indelibly mark them as Christian believers, became more emptied of junk and more filled with the Holy Spirit.

## BE BEING FILLED

Some describing this process of catechesis, which could take many months or even a couple of years, said it was about moving 'from darkness to light.' Like a dimmer switch being slowly turned up as a disciple became progressively less full of dark corners and more and more filled with the light of God.

*Rubbish in Naples. H. Atkins*

So one reason why some of us are not filled with the Spirit now, today, is that we're full of junk – there's no room.

A second reason why we're not filled with the Holy Spirit, and are therefore trying to live the Christian life without the necessary presence and power of God, is that deep down we're scared.

'I don't want to be "possessed,"' we say. Like a person who doesn't drink alcohol much at all, not because they don't like it but because they don't like losing control. And to be honest, language of the Holy Ghost does us no favours in this respect. This very week millions more people will celebrate Halloween as a festival of ghosts, ghouls and paranormal activity than will celebrate the eve of remembering the saints of God – those recognised to be most full of God's Holy Spirit.

I heard this week of one family who had booked a cottage in the middle of nowhere so that the parents can 'treat' their young daughters to a 'proper Halloween experience' – by which they mean staying up most of the night, in a strange house, frightening each other to death! 'Oh, it's all just harmless fun,' we say. And some of it is. All the same, in this modern, sophisticated, unbelieving society, there's many a person who is rightly scared to death.

51

At a particularly terrible time in my own life, long ago now, when my first fiancée became ill and died a handful of months before we planned to marry, I found myself unable to sing that well-known chorus, '*Spirit of the Living God, fall afresh on me.*' I was scared, terrified that God would hear me sing the words 'Break me' – and I felt quite broken enough already. It took me a long time to realise that God was not in the breaking-people-for-destructive-purposes business.

So it's absolutely vital that we realise this. That being filled by the Holy Spirit of God is nothing like being frightened or possessed by an evil force. Rather, to be filled with God's Holy Spirit is to be filled with the presence and nature of God, who is eternal love.

That's why we talk about the Holy Spirit of God in terms of *anointing* – that is, we are enriched and enabled. We're given courage or boldness, either to do something we otherwise couldn't do, or given the strength to walk through circumstances in our lives that we know we simply couldn't cope with in our own strength. This is not 'possession,' it's blessing. '*Take my talents, take my skills, take what's yet to be; let my life be yours, and yet, let it still be me,*' goes the last line of a modern hymn. Yes indeed. Because God doesn't want 'you' obliterated, but rather made pure, holy, more recognisably 'you,' becoming the image of Christ, God's Son.

So one reason why we're not filled with the Spirit is that we're scared. But there's no need to be scared. By God's goodness we're not taken faster than we can go, though sometimes that's faster that we think we can go. The Holy Spirit is the Spirit of Love – and perfect love casts out fear.

Why, you might be pondering at this point, is this sermon titled 'Be Being Filled'? Well, because that's what the text means, here in Acts 10 and so many other places in the New Testament. It's not a one-off event, a single occasion in a distant past. It's an ongoing thing. Because the Holy Spirit encourages and enables us to ever better discipleship of Christ, in word and deed. Think of a car battery. It only charges by being run. Leave your car in the garage for months and you'll save petrol and mileage – and help a little to save the planet. But the battery will go flat by the car not being used. In the same way, Christians who aren't using God's power and resources for the purposes for which God gave them, go flat.

Chinese tea sets are an another example. Some are two hundred years old and in permanent use. Indeed, many say that a very old china teapot is only held together by regularly making tea in it. To stop using it means it dries out and begins to crumble away. With some things, when you stop using it for the purposes it was intended for, it disintegrates.

How often have we heard testimonies like this? 'I received Christ as my Lord and Saviour in May 1977,  and I was filled with the Spirit in 1983. It was wonderful.' I'm sure it was. But just as the best proof of conversion is present convertedness, the best proof of being filled with the Spirit is being full of the Spirit.

So, the more active we are in spiritual terms, in discipleship terms, in our engagement in God's mission of love and service, the more we need to 'be being filled' with the Holy Spirit. Early Methodists were said to be 'greedy for grace.' I guess it's one of the few things it's right to be greedy for. To desire more of God. Today, some of the most wonderful disciples of Christ I know are always the first to say 'Yes' to receiving more of God. Not to squirrel away God's Spirit for a rainy day, or to appear more holy and pious, but to have the power to live out our Christian life, today, now. 'Spirit of the Living God, fall *afresh* on me.' Are you 'be being filled?'

Finally, how will God respond if we ask to 'be being filled'? Whether for the first time, or the thousandth? The passage we read in Luke's gospel gives us the answer. 'If you, bad – evil – as you are know how to give good things to your children,' (and, I suggest, grandchildren!) '*how much more* will your heavenly Father give the Holy Spirit to those who ask him.' You see there are some prayers and heart cries God loves to answer, and 'Please fill me with your Holy Spirit' is one of them. If we pray, 'Lord God, fill us with your Holy Spirit,' God responds, 'I will'.

'I will... but I'm going to have to do some work in you and with you, to remove the junk and clutter first...' We all have two sorts of clutter. Some are the sins we just walk into – usually repeatedly – and with our eyes wide open. Others are what's happened to us. Over which we had little or no control. Yet those things sometimes dominate our lives, like sharp rocks preventing us walking in a lovely pool. Know this today. God can deal with both and wants to deal with both.

And about our fears God says, 'Do not be afraid. I take away fear.' How does that lovely old hymn go? *'For none can guess its grace, till they become the place wherein the Holy Spirit makes his dwelling.'* Even today, now, if chosen.

At Cliff College, the Methodist college where I worked for twelve years, we had an annual celebration event, and thousands used to come for a long weekend. A big banner was strung up between two buildings at the main entry and exit. As you arrived walking upwards on to the site it said, 'Be filled with the Spirit,' and as you left walking downwards away from the site it said, 'Have you been filled with the Holy Spirit?' It's a good question to ask. Today I ask it of us all, remembering that God's readiness to give good gifts to us exceeds our readiness to receive them. Amen.

# 8

# SIGNIFICANT SILENCE

The first of two sermons in this collection preached on Remembrance Sunday, which, given where MCHW is located, is more of an occasion than in many churches. The streets around the building are closed to traffic, open only to the thousands of people attending the Cenotaph, just three hundred yards away. Large numbers of visitors attend the service (particularly if it's raining). The chimes of Big Ben at eleven o'clock, the cannon fire, and the two minute silence itself can all be heard live within the building during morning worship. This particular service was preached in the year marking a century since the end of World War One.

Readings: Psalm 46, James 1:19-25, Revelation 8:1 & Matthew 12:18-21.

On this special year, when we mark one hundred years since the end of the First World War, I want to talk about the significance of silence.

In 2007 I was privileged to attend the service of remembrance at the Cenotaph, taking place right now, very close to us here in Westminster. As the President of the Conference I was the representative of the Methodist Church. I was told what to wear, when to arrive, given pass tickets and went through two bag searches. I met members of the Royal Family, many other eminent people, and the leaders of the other faith communities. It was a well organised, well choreographed event, and I felt honoured to be present.

But without a doubt the poignancy, the gravity of the occasion, hit home when we shared two minutes of silence. When all speaking, all noise stopped. In a world of so many words, and unrelenting noise, the most significant part of a most significant occasion was silence.

But then what would be said? There are some things that occur, that we humans either walk into, or fall into, or run into, or enter on principle, or accident, or mistake, or design, as a gamble, a moral necessity, or a political inevitability, which are so terrible, so traumatic, their effect so pervasive and long-lasting that no words can express or describe them. There are events when there are no adequate words. No words at all. So we keep silent. And the silence speaks more loudly than words.

Today, we mark a complete century on from the ending of the terrible and terrifying events of the Great War, the war to end all wars, it was said. Yet a century during which, we are told, there's not been a single whole day when somewhere, on this small fragile blue planet, human beings have not waged war against each other.

Almost none of us now can actively remember the First World War. A few more of us can actively remember the Second World War, though they too are now getting elderly. Many more of us can remember more recent wars and conflicts, even down to today. But we all know what war does. We all know someone for whom war and conflict has been a life-changing event, to use the jargon of today. We all see its effects. Modern communications technology brings us pictures of people in Syria, Iraq, Afghanistan, South Sudan, Somalia. We look at the images of broken children, bombed houses, gung-ho troops, and we can't speak. We weep quietly. And let the silence express what is felt, deeply. *Significant silence.*

But of course the word 'significant' means something is

signified. The poignant two-minute silence of Armistice Day signifies the moment when the gunfire ceased and the ceasefire started. When peace following war came about. The sheer reality and noise of war drives some people mad. So mad they never fully recover. Those of us who have – thankfully – never actively served in a time of war – can't possibly know what that's like. But even we know, in our comfortable lives, after a time of great stress or testing, or a horrible happening, when we get to the evening, or lay down in bed at night, breathing a big quivering sigh, we can become aware of the silence. And listen to it – for silence can be heard – and recognise its significance. Today, a significant silence marks peace at the end of a war.

But silence also often signifies *death*. When a baby is first born you await a cry, a noise. Because that signifies *life*. I remember some years ago walking in some of those huge graveyards in northern France and Belgium, full of small simple crosses and gravestones, and the large mausoleums that mark the death of thousands of unknown soldiers. It was silent except for the wind. The other people walking round like me were silent. And in that context the silence signified the remembering of death. It's said the silence after Hiroshima was a terrible silence, because of what it signified.

So, silence is significant when those who are alive have no words, but also when there is no one alive to speak at all. *Enforced silence.* Today we remember that significant silence too. For the millions who fell silent. For the hundreds of thousands who still do, year on year in our world today, because of wars and conflicts of various kinds.

There are many occasions in the Bible when the significance of silence is recorded. It's implied in Genesis – the first book in the Bible – when it records that the earth was empty and void, which likely included the absence of sound. But one of the most intriguing is the reference in the last book of the Bible, the book of Revelation. In chapter 8, verse 1 we read,

'*And when he* (that is, the Lord Jesus Christ) *had opened the seventh seal, there was silence in heaven, for about the space of half an hour.*'

The context is relatively straightforward. The Lord Jesus has returned to heaven, victorious. As the conqueror of death and the promiser of life, through his own death and resurrection, he sits on the right hand side of God. He alone has the right to open a book with seven seals, and as they are opened they tell of every sort of evil present on the earth, violence, suffering, war and death. They tell of the day of God's wrath and judgement.

What's this silence in heaven all about? On this poignant day of remembrance I like to think the silence in heaven signifies what our silences signify. We witness the reality of war, and conflict, and other serious things that beset our earth, many of our own human making, and we fall silent. We're appalled. Many are angry – which is another occasion when some of us go silent. And – and this is very important – God is appalled at the things his beloved creatures do to each other, on his good earth. God is angry. So there is silence in heaven.

But perhaps there's silence in heaven for another reason. As the hosts of heaven look upon Jesus Christ, the Lamb who was slain, the Living One who died, they see his sufferings, they realise the cost of final salvation, the price of there being a time, someday, when every tear will be wiped away and all things are made new. And as they – and as we – realise the emotion of God, the involvement of God in the world God created, the extent of God's love made plain in the sacrifice of his only Son, there is silence. They – we – are awestruck.

There is silence in heaven as a sense of wonder – of awe – comes about. Wonder and awe about two different things.

First, *awful* wonder at *suffering*. Because one of the great significances of silence is an acknowledgement of suffering. In the Old Testament book of Job we read of a devout man who God permits to go through various trials and sufferings.

# SIGNIFICANT SILENCE

Many chapters record Job receiving the verbal wisdom of his 'comforters,' three friends. But in one verse we read this: *'And they sat with him on the ground seven days and seven nights, and no one spoke a word to him, for they saw that his suffering was very great.'*

Second, *awesome* wonder at the *continuing love of God*, who in spite of everything will not give up on a rebellious, warring, jealous, combative humanity which is so much less than God created it to be. In heaven, in spite of everything – everything we have been through and everything we have yet to go through – God's love and will for our healing, our peace, our *shalom*, remains. In that wonderful, abiding love is, ultimately, our hope, causing

*Growth in hard ground. H. Atkins*

us to live up to – rather than down to – who we really are: those lovingly created in the image of God; the race for whom Christ, the Son of God, laid down his own life – that we might live.

Is silence always golden? No. On this day of significant silences, there's the proper call not to always keep silent. To protest for peace. To speak out against injustices. To shout down evil. To be heard in the defence of those who are victims. So the last significant silence we note today is the resolve to hear those who speak out for what is right, to join them, live out their challenges, to repudiate all that is contrary to God's way, all that cheapens human life, and continue the long, hard, but ultimately right road, towards true peace. Amen.

# 9

# WAYMARKS

This was the first sermon I preached at MCHW as Superintendent minister, and it was consequently preached at the start of a new Methodist year. It draws heavily on the pilgrim route to Santiago de Compostela – the Camino. I wore my Camino shell like a pectoral cross as I preached, and I had ready hundreds of scallop shells in baskets at the front of the sanctuary. At the end of the sermon I invited people to come and choose a shell, declaring their desire to be pilgrims at a time of new beginnings, as we continued to walk the ancient routes of our faith.

Reading: Luke 24:13-35.

Don't you just love the story of the Emmaus Road? It's normally a reading for the Easter season, but I chose it today as it's a journey story and we are beginning a new chapter of our journeying as disciples of Christ here at Methodist Central Hall, Westminster.

Luke loves journeys! They're everywhere in his writings, both in his gospel and in the Acts of the Apostles, which is really one long journey story. And when you're on a journey in Luke, there's a high chance that God is going to show up in a special way. Luke records Jesus telling stories about journeys that no other gospel writer does. Of prodigals leaving home, travelling and returning – because a journey is a time when some of us come to our senses and realise what's what. Of a good Samaritan, who found a bit of beat up humanity on the road belonging to a group deeply disliked for various cultural, historical and sociological reasons, and ministered to him with kindness and generosity. Because journeys provide opportunities to encounter others and choose what sort of people we will be. It's Luke who tells us that Saul of Tarsus was on a journey to Damascus when God broke into his life and turned it upside down, and the sworn enemy of Christ's followers becomes Paul, the great apostle of the faith. Because journeys change lives and how they are lived out.

Then there's this story, the walk to Emmaus, when the risen Jesus draws near to two bewildered, sad disciples – perhaps a man and wife – and comforts, challenges, teaches and then disappears. And despondent disciples are transformed into joyful ones. When we're on a journey, Luke declares, we encounter God in many and wonderful ways.

Which is perhaps why many Christians go on pilgrimage. A few years ago I walked the last few hundred kilometres of the pilgrim route to Santiago de Compostela with my wife Helen and some friends. Known as the Camino, it's an ancient pilgrimage starting just inside southern France and going across northern Spain to its western tip, ending at the shrine of St. James – Santiago. It was a wonderful, meaningful, transformative journey.

All along the route there are waymarks. Many are stone pillars, others are built into walls, or are beautiful mosaics on the road you walk. They literally mark the way. Some are ancient and some quite new. All bear the scallop-shaped shell – the sign of the Camino pilgrim – and lots of new ones also have bright yellow arrows, to prevent you from going the wrong way.

*Waymark on the Camino. H. Atkins*

There are people from all over the world on the Camino. Some go alone and some travel together – often having never met before but forming a little group. Some go fast, some slow. Some talk a lot, some want solitude.

As you talk to those you meet you quickly realise that people are walking the Camino for many reasons. One person we met had a heavy rucksack which, he explained, was part-filled with rocks. This was the weight of his sin, he said, and he was walking the Camino as an atonement for them. I would love to think that like St. Paul, he encountered Jesus who wonderfully forgave him, and took his sins away, so he walked light and free along that road. Another person we met had been healed and wanted to thank God by praising and praying her way along the road, and sharing what had happened to her.

Some pilgrims simply walk past the waymarks, which count down the distance to Santiago. But many use them as stopping places. For a rest. A conversation. Or for worship, as we did, reading a psalm, singing a hymn, saying a prayer.

You've probably already noticed, but all the things that happen on Luke's journeys still happen today as you walk the way of a pilgrim. Some of us are prodigals. We are either heading away from home and family or returning to them. Some of us 'come to our senses.' Some of us identify with the characters in the Good Samaritan story. Some have been beaten up by life, and others look out for those beaten up by life and care for them. Some of us, like St. Paul, have quite a past, but experience God on the road. We are blind, and then we see. All of us finish the journey different people to the person who started out.

Some of us, like the two on the road to Emmaus, walk sad, bewildered, questioning what's happened, and become aware that the Jesus we thought was missing is in fact walking along with us. We don't always see it at first, but through the fellowship of the road the penny drops, and bread is broken, and we come to a new place of faith. And the wonderful thing is that Jesus Christ still draws near, still comforts, still challenges, still heals, still restores, still turns lives upside down – so that they are the right way up! Some of us, for the first or hundred and first time, need to hear that good news today. The Lord wants to walk with you, now, today.

You may have noticed the shell I'm wearing. It's a scallop shell and it's the symbol of the Camino pilgrimage to the shrine of St James. Lots of those walking to Santiago de Compostela have them. To carry or wear one is to declare, in effect, 'I'm a pilgrim and I'm on a pilgrim journey.'

As a congregation, we've reached a new waymark today. Our past road of over a hundred years, born in the generosity of others and a deep desire that people called Methodists be here at the heart of one of the great cities of the world, has taken us past many waymarks, highs and lows, rain and shine, laughter and tears. And now at the start of a new Methodist year – another year of God's constant, covenant love and amazing grace – with a changed leadership and staff team, with folk well established and folk new to our fellowship, we pause at another waymark.

Might we sing a little Charles Wesley at this waymark? '*Why hast thou cast our lot in the same age and place, and why together brought to see each other's face? ... Didst thou not make us one, that we might one remain, together travel on and share our joy and pain...*'

Over the next period of time we will journey together, a family of Christ's disciples. At any point in time some of us will be sad and despondent, and others rejoicing. Some will feel far from God and others drawn nearer than ever. Some will be Good Samaritans and others the person beaten up. Some of us will identify with the Emmaus road couple – at every point in the journey story. But we have been given each other for this part of the pilgrimage, and – even better still – the Lord will be with us. There's an East African saying: 'If you want to travel fast, go alone. If you want to travel far, go together.' So today, at this waymark point, I invite you to take up a shell, the symbol of a pilgrim, and resolve to walk together as disciples of Jesus, as individuals and as a church community. Amen.

# 10

# CAN I USE YOUR BOAT?

A sermon originally written for Cliff College students on completion of their studies, many of them going into Christian ministries of various kinds, which is probably still its most appropriate context. Here, amended for 'general consumption,' it focuses on God's call and some simple lessons applied by use of phrases found in the text. It was preached at MCHW in the context of commissioning a group of members volunteering for service in the West London Winter Night Shelter ministry.

Reading: Luke 5:1-11.

I want to continue a theme that we've focused on in recent weeks, about the call of God on our lives. Today we turn to Luke chapter 5, to one of the stories found in the gospels about Jesus calling his first disciples.

One of my former colleagues used to wear varifocal glasses. When he was speaking he used to tell his hearers, 'The top part of the lens is for seeing long distance, the bottom part is for close reading, and the middle part is for seeing right through you!' As we look at this passage we'll occasionally look at it from 'long distance,' seeing the wider context, then sometimes very specifically. But as we do so we need to remember that every time we study the Scriptures, the Holy Spirit is studying us, looking right through us, always with the intention of calling and enabling us to deeper discipleship of Jesus.

Now, Luke sets this story in the context of the growing popularity of Jesus. Jesus needs helpers, and this is how he goes about choosing and appointing them. We use several quotations from the text to help us focus.

*Chinese rope boat, Guangdong province, China. H. Atkins*

'*Jesus got into one of the boats, the one belonging to Peter...*' Jesus is saying, in effect, 'Peter, can I use *your* boat? Can I use you, who you are and what you do, what you possess and know?'

So often we think being called by God means that all that we are and know is washed away, irrelevant, that God always begins his work in us on a clean piece of paper. Not so. 'Can I use your boat?' asks Christ of each of us. Can I use you, all of you – what you have and know and are – for my glory and purposes? And if you say 'Yes,' he transforms it. Water turns into wine. Fishers of fish become fishers of people. Disciples often chose their rabbis, but Jesus chooses his disciples.

'*The fishermen had gone out of the boats and were washing their nets.*' I want you to note that Jesus sometimes calls people to follow him at the most inappropriate moments! These men normally fish in the half-light or dark. In the daytime they're resting or doing jobs relating to fishing. So mending nets in the morning is absolutely right. It means you can sit in the sun, listening to preachers, and they surely heard Jesus teach and preach as they worked. So when Jesus says to Simon, 'Can I use your boat?' – it's at a bad time. It is, to all intents and purposes, a wrong time. It's a time when they're not ready. A time when you wouldn't expect them to be ready. It's a time for mending nets, a time for getting married, for child-rearing, and job hunting, a time for career-chasing and 101 other perfectly legitimate things.

But you see the *really* right time, as the miraculous catch of fish demonstrates, is the time Jesus calls. Some of you may be wrestling with a call from God and are ignoring it because you think it's the wrong time. You may be right, but then again, that's sometimes the time God does call.

I want you to note too that Jesus who calls Peter is interested in the *whole of his life*, not just the religious bits or the practical ways in which Peter can serve him. If we'd started our reading a few verses earlier, in the last few verses of Luke 4, we'd note that Jesus has been to Simon's house and while there has healed his mother-in-law. So this isn't the first time they've met. Jesus engages with Peter's domestic family situation, then his work situation, then calls Peter to follow him. So with us. Being called to follow Jesus doesn't mean that his only interest in us is in terms of our becoming a preacher or offering religious service, as if that's your only worth to him. Jesus desires to be invited into every aspect of our life, not just the religious bits. And if that's how Jesus deals with his disciples, then and now, then we, as his disciples today, mustn't limit our own commitment and interest simply to the 'religious bits' of other people's lives. The whole gospel relates to the whole of human life.

'*Put out into the deep water,*' says Jesus. There's a silly story of a man drowning. 'Help me!' he shouts. Suddenly there's a splash beside him and he flings his arms round the person in the water. 'Thank you, thank you,' he sobs, 'you've come to rescue me!' 'No,' comes the reply. 'I can't swim either, I just thought you might like some company!' Well that's not quite what I mean when I urge us to go out into deeper waters! By deeper waters I mean following Jesus in ways that you can't always 'touch the bottom.' To trust beyond what you see. To not be in complete control. To know that it's all right that you can't touch the bottom. Sometimes we exercise such lack of faith. We want to know what it will be like to follow Christ – what exactly will we do, where will we be going, how much will we be earning, and so on. But when you are called to follow Jesus, you don't call the shots. So don't ask for it all cut and dried. Step out beyond your depth, because Jesus calls us to where we aren't always in charge. So many of us play around in the shallows of our faith, but don't be content with that. After all, you never fully know you can truly swim unless you go out into deep waters.

So the fishermen go out into deep waters and fish. I don't want to dwell on this point in this sermon, but we should just note in passing that obedience to Jesus bears fruit. *'If you say so, I will let down the nets.'*

And what a catch! *'So they signalled to their partners in the other boat to come and help them.'* The next lesson from this passage is this: don't be a one-person band. Have you noticed how often champions, whether tennis players after the winning forehand or golfers after the winning put, run straight to their loved ones and their support team? Because they know that their successes are never achieved alone. So it is in terms of our Christian discipleship. One of the most common weaknesses of those who follow Christ, particularly into positions of leadership and responsibility, is that they become a one man – or woman – band. So we need to notice the partnerships in this story. Those in the other boat are invited to help bring in the large catch of fish. Disciples, together, involved in the fruit of being obedient to Jesus.

In my experience, Jesus rarely calls people into solo ministry or service of any kind. Does Jesus choose Peter, James and John as three individuals? Yes. But he also calls them as the 'Galilee Fishermen Inc.', effectively taking over a family firm. And it's this team of three within the larger group of disciples with him on the Mount of Transfiguration. They'd worked together and relied upon each other long before being called into the band of disciples.

# CAN I USE YOUR BOAT?

Jesus calls you to follow, but he doesn't necessarily call you to be alone.

At the huge catch of fish Simon falls at Jesus' knees and says, *'Go away from me, Lord, for I am a sinful man!'* I wonder how you respond to God working in your life. Make no mistake; it is a heavy thing sometimes. It's wonderful. But it also often involves a sense of awe. Me – little me – called to be an agent of the Lord of heaven and earth. Fortunately, Jesus doesn't 'go away' from Peter, as he asks, any more than Jesus departs from us. Instead, Jesus says, *'Do not be afraid.'* Because Jesus doesn't always do what you ask him, but his response to us is always exactly right. Peter doesn't say, 'Why didn't I know where the fish were?' He falls at Jesus' feet. Peter's skills are not at issue here, but his obedience and trust in Jesus are. Whatever your sense of call in Christian ministries might be, ask the Holy Spirit to make you a person who does not focus on counting the fish, but one who falls at the feet of the master.

*'Do not be afraid; from now on you will be catching people,'* says Jesus. *'When they had brought their boats to shore, they left everything and followed him.'* 'Follow me' isn't a Christian version of a party game! It combines what you used to do – fish for fish, or whatever – with what you now know you must do – follow Christ and do what he asks of you. There's always continuity and discontinuity in God's calls to us.

And 'Follow me' is also always relational. It is, "Follow *me.*" Not, note, learn about Christianity, do a college course, become an expert theologian, or become a minister or a youth worker or whatever. All Christians are disciples first, *then* whatever God calls them to be and do. We are not called to follow a call, but to follow Christ. So we go: in God's strength, seeking to do God's will as disciples of Christ. May the Lord guide and keep us all. Amen.

# 11

# GOD'S KINGDOM PEOPLE

Preached shortly after the completion of a major refurbishment of the chapel at MCHW and as we approached a period of significant ministerial staff changes. The sermon attempts to gently remind the congregation of the primacy of the kingdom of God in and through its life and witness.

Readings: 1 Corinthians 4:16-20 & Matthew 5:1-12.

The first words of Jesus recorded in Mark's gospel are these: '*The kingdom of God is at hand. Repent and believe the good news!*' The 'kingdom of God' – or 'kingdom of heaven' in Matthew – is the central theme of Jesus' teaching recorded in all the gospels. So I thought we'd spend a little time reflecting on God's kingdom today.

There's one key point and several corollaries – things that flow from it. The key point is this:

*It's God's kingdom – not ours.* When the disciples ask Jesus how to pray and he teaches them what we call the Lord's Prayer, we're not told to say 'Our kingdom come,' or '*My* kingdom come,' but '*Thy* kingdom come.' It's God's kingdom and those who seek to be Christ's followers need to know and remember that. It's an obvious point, but the corollaries of taking that seriously are enormous. We look at a few.

First, if it's God's kingdom, then *the Church is God's kingdom community.* When the Church worships, it's being a kingdom community. No Christian community can be a kingdom community if it doesn't worship God – Father, Son and Holy Spirit. When the Church breaks bread together it's being a kingdom community, because it's doing what Jesus its Lord told it to do. When the Church proclaims grace, or mercy, or justice, it is being a kingdom community, and so on.

But there's a danger. It's this. The Church and God's kingdom become interchangeable in our thinking. We think that Church as we know it, as we run it, as it presently is, IS the kingdom of God. Which is the wrong way round. Because if Christ's Church is not being and doing the things of the kingdom of God, God doesn't say, 'OK, I'll rethink what my kingdom is like.' No. God requires those of us who pray 'Your kingdom come' to be Church that fits the nature of the kingdom, not the other way round.

Down the centuries there's been a constant tussle between the life and traditions of the Church, and what's proclaimed as the kingdom of God. The 19th century theologian Alfred Loisy lamented, 'Jesus came proclaiming the kingdom, and what arrived was the Church.' Attending church, belonging to a church, is too readily assumed to be living in God's kingdom. When in fact it might not be. In the last year we've refurbished both our fellowship meeting room and our chapel – at a significant cost, requiring generous giving from many in this congregation. They're lovely spaces, but we haven't brought God's kingdom any nearer unless what goes on in them glorifies and proclaims and embodies the kingdom of God.

Please don't misunderstand me. The Church is a great blessing. Our church is a great blessing. But it's not the whole focus or expression of the kingdom. Perhaps it's a fuelling station for the work of the kingdom. John Wesley once famously said, 'I regard the whole world as my parish.' Christians who love *their* church too much – in a way that suggests that 'this is ours,' that we own it, that it must do what we want and how we want it – fall time and again into acting as if 'the parish was our whole world.' So Christian disciples are required to undertake 'the kingdom test,' a bit like we periodically have our blood pressure taken. Otherwise a 'go to' Faith becomes a 'come to' church.

So to summarise: a key fact of the kingdom of God is that it's God's – not ours; and if so then the Church is first and foremost God's kingdom community – not ours, and consequently – our next thought – *God chooses who is admitted to the kingdom, and on what basis – not us.*

*'Jesus came preaching, "The kingdom of God is at hand, repent and believe the good news."'*

Recently, we were challenged from a heckler in the congregation to be clear about what happens to those who reject Christ, those who don't repent and believe. The New Testament suggests that such people place themselves in darkness, choosing not to receive the light that God offers to all. They place themselves outside God's desire and will for them. The New Testament says that if we don't receive and honour Jesus in this life, we won't be received and honoured in the next. And so on.

A key issue with preaching hellfire and damnation, however, is that it is not what Jesus Christ primarily teaches. Jesus preaches the kingdom of God, and asks his people to do likewise. I recall a conversation with an American preacher at *Easter People.* I'd been preaching earlier that evening and was now sat in the hotel lounge, and got talking to the preacher from the night before, a nice man, a pastor from one of the Baptist denominations in the United States. Apropos of nothing he suddenly said, 'You Methodists really want people to get to heaven, don't you?' I was completely nonplussed but said, 'Yes, don't all Christians?' 'I guess,' he replied, 'but my church seems to spend more time telling people what it's like in hell rather than urging them to get to heaven.'

Do you see? Our doctrine of evangelism doesn't determine God's plans for humankind. Our preaching doesn't decisively mark out who belongs in the kingdom of God and who doesn't.

What we're asked to be about by our Lord is to be like him, in word and deed, and his deeds and words were about God's kingdom.

The picture in the book of Revelation – of people coming from the east and west and north and south to sing the praises of the Lamb, whom God has set on the throne of the kingdom – is wonderful but so challenging. Why? Because of the sheer range and variety of those who are there. In fact they hold only one thing in common. They have made Jesus Christ their Lord and sought to follow him. And in so doing, they have connected themselves, mind soul and body, to the purposes of the King of the kingdom.

Remember that old joke? Jesus is showing people round heaven and as they come to a room with the door closed he goes, 'Shush.' 'Why?' 'That's the very strict and particular Methodists, they think they're the only ones here!' The kingdom of heaven is going to be full of faces we know. And many of us who have lost loved ones are so looking forward to somehow – in some way not fully known, but in trust wholly hoped for – being reunited. But the kingdom of heaven is also going to be full of people we don't know. We'll possibly be askance: 'What are they doing here?' And Jesus, the Lord of heaven and earth will say, 'Because I died for them and invited them too.'

So... it's God's kingdom, and therefore the Church is God's not ours, and therefore God invites into the kingdom whom God wants, not us... and – lastly – therefore, we are expected to live according to the laws of the kingdom.

An American pastor friend Steve Manskar makes this point tellingly. He recounts the well-known story of the prodigal son, then asks what happened next – which of course Luke doesn't tell us about. He imagines the father rousing his somewhat hungover son early the next morning and telling him to get up because there's work to be done! After the party is the work of the kingdom. '*Repent and believe the Good News,*' says Jesus. We don't necessarily have to *like* it all! In the last years of his life my dear old dad used a stick. A telescopic one. I remember helping him in and out the car and the number of times he couldn't lengthen it or shorten it, the number of times it got stuck in the car door, and he'd say, 'I hate this stick,' then he'd pause and say, 'but it stops me from falling over.'

God doesn't say, 'I love you' – full stop. Nothing else. The declaration of God's love, the initial realisation of God's saving grace is a beginning, not an end. There's always something more. That's why we emphasise growth in the Spirit, renewal of faith, more prayer, better Bible study, godlier worship, deeper sacramentality.

But there's even more. Which is where – late in the day, I know – I turn briefly to our readings.

First, the beatitudes. *'Blessed are the peacemakers, for they will be called children of God… Blessed are those who are persecuted for righteousness' sake, for theirs is the kingdom of heaven… Blessed are those who hunger and thirst for righteousness, for they will be filled,'* and so on. Do you know that only the kingdom of God runs on righteousness? All other kingdoms run on oil, or military might, or subjugation, or exploitation, or hedonism, or wealth creation… only God's kingdom runs on righteousness. So note, please, how the Beatitudes describe what God's kingdom is like and what God's kingdom people are like. Don't you think that today, with the world as it is, with this country at the point in time it is, with the Christian Church as it is, and with you and me as we are, this is teaching for us today?

Then, second, in 1 Corinthians we read, *'For the kingdom of God is not a matter of talk but of power.'* John Wesley famously said, 'Give me one hundred people who fear nothing but sin and desire nothing but God, and I care not whether they be clergy or laity, they alone will shake the gates of Hell *and set up the kingdom of Heaven upon Earth.'*

I close. How do I – little me – help bring the kingdom of God on earth? First, I need to place myself under Christ's lordship again, now, whether for the first or the thousandth time. Second, I need to recognise that in doing so I'm co-opted to be a partner in making God's kingdom come, now, here, where I am. Third, in order to do that I must recognise it's God's kingdom not mine; that the church I love and belong to is God's, not mine; and that God is in charge of who comes into the kingdom, and how, not me. And that it will be made

*Lady with placard. H. Atkins*

clear how serious I am about all this by how I live by the rules of the kingdom, to what extent I am shaped by the teaching of Christ, in word and deed. Nobody said it was easy. But there's no more significant or better challenge offered to us in the whole of our life. Are you in? I hope so. Amen.

# 12

# WHAT A CHURCH!

A sermon of three conversion stories. The basic idea and a good number of the insights in this sermon arose from sharing an event with Chip Freed, a United Methodist Pastor in Ohio, who being a gracious soul readily agreed I borrow his ideas!

Reading: Acts 16:6-34, read in three parts relating to the three stories, at the appropriate point in the sermon.

I want us to look at three conversion stories, all found in Acts 16. The conversion stories are of Lydia, a rich businesswoman, a slave girl being trafficked as a fortune teller, and a jailor, a working man.

First Lydia, about whom we're told a number of things. She's a businesswoman, a trader, in expensive purple cloth – the dye coming from crushing a rare seashell found in the coastal area around Thyatira, in the modern Turkey, which is where she's originally from. So she's a foreigner, an immigrant, and may well be a widow. By implication, she's wealthy. She certainly has a house and household able to accommodate all the missionary party. She's described as 'a worshipper of God,' probably meaning she believes in the One True God of the Jews but isn't a full convert to Judaism.

But let's go backwards in time a little. Paul had intended to go east – incidentally, to the region Lydia came from – but the Holy Spirit said 'No.' Part of God's way of saying 'No' is that Paul has a vision of a Macedonian man saying, 'Come over and help us.' So Paul goes west, not east, and the earlier verses in Acts 16 describe the journey and how the small group of Christians land by ship and then walk to Philippi.

On the Sabbath, Paul and the others set off to go to where the Jews meet for worship. However, instead of a synagogue – which he might've been expecting to find – he comes across a group of women, meeting for prayer. Some say this suggests that there wasn't the required number of Jewish males – ten – to formally create a synagogue in Philippi, making clear its dominant paganism. No doubt introductions were made, and the women invite Paul to speak. We don't have the text of his sermon but we do know that Lydia responded to the gospel. The text says, 'The Lord opened her heart' to what was said, which is a way of saying that she 'got it.' Just as we might listen to sermons for years, but suddenly 'get it'! Lydia then invites them to her home. She and her household are baptised, and at the end of chapter 16 we're told her home has become the first Christian church in Philippi.

I want you to notice that. The first thing Lydia, the new convert does, is open her home. Where God opens hearts, God opens homes, spaces, even our church. People who have been accepted become accepting. A key element of saving grace is hospitality. I can't stress how powerful a witness and ministry is a hospitable Christian home, and a hospitable Christian congregation! Open doors. Inviting spaces. Non-judgemental environments. Places of hospitality and sanctuary. These are signs that a gracious God has moved in our lives. How evident are they in our homes, and our churches?

Let's briefly take stock. The Lord brings Lydia from the east, from Turkey, to Philippi in the west. The Lord tells Paul who wanted to go east to Turkey to go west, and he comes to Philippi.

The Lord brings them together and Lydia is saved, and her hospitality causes Paul to perhaps continue to rethink his attitudes about hospitality – and possibly about women! If you'd asked Paul, when on the boat, if his aim was to start a church with a group of women, he'd have probably laughed. And I wonder at what point Paul realised that his 'Macedonian man' was an 'Asian woman"!

Then there's the *slave girl*, a soothsayer, a fortune teller, with an evil spirit. The Greek text describes her having a 'python spirit,' as in a snake, probably referring to the ornate snake sculpture that guarded the Delphic Oracle in central Greece. The Greek god Apollo was said to have killed the actual snake, and its ability to predict the future then entered the high priestess and spread to others, particularly women. So possessing a python spirit – or being possessed by a python spirit – probably both - meant that the girl was said to be able to tell the future, and this gift was exploited by her owners to make them a fortune – she was effectively being trafficked.

The girl follows Paul and the others about, exclaiming to all and sundry, 'These men are servants of the Most High God and proclaiming the way of salvation.' And of course that's true. In which case, was she doing them a favour – telling the truth about them? Or was she being sarcastic? Did her words assist their mission or hamper it? We don't know. What we do know is that Paul got sick and tired of it, and angry. The Greek word used in the text implies that Paul had a number of complex emotions. He's *aggravated* by her shouting (remember how you felt when your baby just wouldn't stop screaming?) and *angry* about the situation. But he's also *grieved* about the situation the girl finds herself in, her captivity, exploitation and abuse. And he's *saddened* that she was in bondage. Well, double bondage really: bound to the evil spirit and also bound to evil traffickers. It's with this complicated combination of emotions that Paul had had enough and casts the evil spirit out of her. And Paul's exorcism worked. Otherwise the girl's owners wouldn't have grabbed Paul and Silas and dragged them off to the courts to complain. They are incandescent! Paul has killed their golden goose!

We don't know for certain if the girl was converted and joined the church at Lydia's place. I like to think she did, and the fact that her story is sandwiched between two people who are soundly converted, suggests she did. If so, what a great church Lydia led! Because we're witnessing someone who enters Christian fellowship with lots of 'baggage' and 'history,' who has some way to travel to receive saving grace. At first all the girl knows is that her life has been changed and this group of people have something to do with it. And slowly she draws a little closer: to them and to Christ. Do you know that our churches are blessed when we have such folk among us? That some of us can only move nearer Christ and his Church slowly, inch by inch, because of what has happened to us? Could a converted, abused, possessed girl find a place, be accepted in our church? Are we patient enough? Understanding enough? Forgiving enough? Thick-skinned enough? Pray God we are.

The *jailor* was probably ex-military. A hard man. He could take prisoners with their backs bleeding, throw them into prison, fasten their feet into stocks, lock the door and go get a good night's sleep. And in prison, and in pain, and in shackles, Paul and Silas are singing at midnight. Praise to God and hope in Christ!

Let's just pause here a moment. We so often behave as if simple setbacks spell an end. Give it up! How much, in the comfy, replete, un-persecuted West, do we have to learn about the doggedness of faith and hope!

Then there's the earthquake! The earth moving is the clincher. The jailor releases Paul and Silas and cries out, 'What must I do to be saved?' And Paul leads him to Christ – a man who only hours earlier will have sworn at him, spat on him, ridiculed him, beaten him up and treated him as less than nothing. Now that's grace!

And note this. That when the jailor is saved, the first thing he does is wash the apostles' wounds. Remember what I said about hospitality? Besides praying and reading the Bible, the early Methodists – a name of ridicule, remember – started pharmacies, visited those in prison, walked with them to the gallows. Because care, and tending, and compassion are the fruits of grace. It's not done simply in order to save people. It's done because you're saved.

Then the man and his family are baptised – like Lydia was. Just think. Given the absence of a lot of water Paul may have baptised the man in the common bowl the man had just used to tend Paul's wounds! The jailor washed them – and was then washed. Sanctifying, sustaining grace has begun.

*Bun cakes for Christian Aid week. H. Atkins*

Well, have you heard the one about the rich woman, the slave girl and the jailor? It sounds like a joke! But notice how these three conversions are so deliberately different.

They're *racially* different. Lydia is Asian – and therefore a migrant in Philippi, a cosmopolitan Greek-influenced Roman city. The slave girl is 'nothing' but comes from the pagan world, and the jailor is almost certainly a Roman citizen.

They're *economically* different. Lydia is rich and respectable, the slave girl owns nothing, and the jailor is an ordinary working family man.

The *circumstances* in which they encounter the Lord are different. Lydia was at a prayer meeting, the slave girl was on the streets, and the jailer was doing his job.

They're *psychologically* different. Lydia is a cognitive type – 'Explain to me the gospel,' she says. The slave girl is *experiential*, requiring a clear, supernatural experience of God that makes sense

81

to her. The jailor needs something practical. 'If you'd escaped,' he says, 'I'd have had to kill myself.'

They're at different points in a *spiritual* journey. Lydia is clearly seeking God. The slave girl is clearly serving Satan, and the jailor is – like so many people today – clearly unshaped by any notion of religion. He's just doing his job, until he comes across Paul and Silas.

And yet. And yet they responded to the same gospel and were received into the same church. You see the gospel of grace is for everybody.

Wouldn't you just love to be a fly on the wall of the church in Philippi at Lydia's house? What a holy mess! Like the young lad who joined the fellowship and in a time of testimony exclaimed enthusiastically to the group, 'I think you and God are just f**king brilliant!' Because lost people act lost. And broken people act broken. Look at the diversity of the church – the only common factor is Christ. But church for everybody can change anybody. And that's what this passage is about!

The gospel of Jesus Christ – and the Church that arises from it – is the most potent vehicle in the world to bring different people together. Lord, forgive us that so often we are not! And that we do not!

In Paul's many letters to churches he's not always warm and cuddly! Some churches get a real flea in their ear! So when, much later in time, Paul writes to the church in Philippi, what does he say? '*I thank my God every time I remember you…*' He writes to a healthy church without criticism.

A final word about Paul, and about change and grace in Paul himself. Because like all followers of Jesus, God is teaching new things. It's the same for us. Holiness is a continuing openness to learn of God, trust in Christ and be obedient to the Holy Spirit. And growth in grace and holiness comes about as much in the mess of human life as in the more 'normal' markers of holiness such as prayer, reading the Scriptures, sharing fellowship and availing yourself of means of grace.

## WHAT A CHURCH!

Paul was a Jew. A strict Jew. A Pharisee, who like millions of Jews then – and some even now – prayed every day a prayer like this: 'I thank you Lord that you have not made me a Gentile, you have not made me a woman and that you have not made me a slave.' And at the clear leading of the Holy Spirit of God, in pagan Philippi, a healthy church is started with a wealthy woman, a redeemed slave and a gentile working man! What a gospel! What a church! Let's be more like it! Amen.

# 13

# PSALMS, HYMNS AND SPIRITUAL SONGS

Each year MCHW hosts Daffodil Day. It's effectively a spring rally, historically for women but increasingly now men also attend. Though a little quaint it serves an important role in encouraging and bolstering the faith of hugely loyal folk, many belonging to quite small and often somewhat tired, elderly congregations. Guest singers perform, celebrities appear, the great organ is expertly played, and hymns and songs are sung loudly and lustily by the circa 1,800 attenders. And of course a speaker speaks. For about ten minutes. This is one such short sermon, and I sang (rather than spoke) all the hymns and choruses used in it.

Reading: Colossians 3:14-17.

Well, you're all in fine voice today! Of course we Methodists put great store on what we sing. Born in Song, Singing the Faith, and all that. The importance of hymns – those weighty, beautiful, articulate, moving and profound pieces of congregational singing – often express what we feel and believe better than we can ever say simply in words.

I can still remember the first time I sang 'And Can It Be.' It was with several hundred others at a big rally in 1972. A tingle went down my spine, and I thought, 'This is what it's going to be like in heaven.' Later, I came to realise that what I sang with others not only said what I believed but also *increased* my belief. As I sang I knew that I belonged with these people, God's people, this was our faith *and* mine. Do you know what I mean?

When I was the Secretary of the Methodist Conference I occasionally got letters from people wanting to change the hymns we sing at the conference when we remember and give thanks for ministers, missionaries and local preachers who had died during the year. I'm afraid it was at that point that this modern-song loving, fresh expressions supporting, renewal-encouraging minister wrote back – politely of course – 'No. Not on my watch!' I mean, what do you put in place of Wesleys, 'Come, let us join our friends above that have obtained the prize'? To sing, remembering the faithful gone before us, 'O that we might grasp our Guide! O that the word were given! Come, Lord of hosts the waves divide, and land us all in heaven.'

Then there are spiritual songs. When I worked at Cliff College, I met folk who said that it was worship songs and old choruses that kept their faith alive. 'Turn your eyes upon Jesus, look full in his wonderful face, and the things of earth will grow strangely dim in the light of his glory and grace.' Remember? For me, becoming a Christian in the early 1970s it was Youth Praise 1 and 2. The green book and the orange book. 'For me to live is Christ, to die is gain, to hold his hand and walk his narrow way. There is no peace no joy no fill, like walking in his will, for me to live is Christ to die is gain.' Remember? These songs of worship – whether older chorus or new worship song – also express what we believe. Like classic hymns, they deepen our faith. They root us in the community of the faithful. They help shape who, at our best, we are.

I have two memories I want to share. The first is from Cuba when I was there for a few weeks in late 2005 teaching a crash course to about two hundred young adults called to ministry in the wonderful renewal of the Methodist Church taking place there. It was the only time in my life I've knowingly shared my bed with a scorpion – but not for long! While there, I went to a village in the jungle to preach and found a community rebuilding their houses following a tornado which had flattened the whole place a few weeks earlier. On return from work all the people gathered each evening and built a simple house. A family moved in and they started the next one. And as they rebuilt the flattened houses they sang hymns. There was something profoundly moving about standing in a recently devastated village, where in many cases everything a family owned had been blown away, and as they rebuilt their lives they sang songs of praise to God. Perhaps it's at times like that, that you realise the real gift of hymns and psalms and spiritual songs – that what has been poured into you down the years, pours out of you at moments of crisis.

My second memory is more recent and personal, and I hope you don't mind me sharing it. My parents are still alive but old and virtually housebound. Faithful Christian souls but increasingly frail. My mother fell, my dad tried to lift her, he fell, gashed his hand open, and they rang Helen, my wife. I was out of the country, and Helen went over to a disaster scene and ferried them both off to hospital. They queued in A&E, and got put together in a small bay, side by side awaiting assessment, cold, bewildered, no doubt frightened. My dad – not the most spiritually vocal person in the world – started singing, 'Here I am, Lord...' at four o'clock in the morning, and a nurse pulled back the plastic screen and said, 'Well, someone's chirpy in here.' Chirpy? Maybe. Better to say he was not only singing the faith, but he was singing his faith.

On a day like this, that's a key question. Are we still singing our faith, or just singing? One response to God we might make today is to say to God, 'Lord, today, I believe. This stuff we sing, by your grace has entered my soul, and shaped it, and made me who I am. Thank you. I still believe it and I still love and trust you.'

Many of you will have heard the marvellous story of the young man who was diagnosed with a brain tumour, and because of the nature of the operation he underwent he had to remain awake throughout, so the surgical team asked him to sing to signal that he was still conscious, still well, still alive. He chose '10,000 Reasons (Bless the Lord),' the song we're going to sing as we draw to a close. Because, said the young man, if the operation goes wrong, and I die, I'll still be singing this song in heaven. As will we. Praise God! Amen.

# 14

# WHOSE IS IT?

A sermon for Harvest.

Readings: Genesis 2:4-9, 15-17 & 1 Corinthians 6:19-20.

When I was young – a long time ago now! – and I was using one of my dad's tools, which I often did, and I didn't clean it, or put it back in the right place, or leave it outside in the rain to rust, he'd say something like this: 'You can do what you like with your own things, but this isn't yours. I don't mind you borrowing it, but if you use it you must use it properly and look after it.' And if I'd been misusing particularly fine or expensive tools he'd say, 'These things don't grow on trees you know!'

On the occasion of our Harvest we can easily imagine those words spoken to us by our Creator, about how we use this world. Our Harvest thanksgiving is a good time to reflect on the issue of *ownership* and *the treatment of things.*

Well, whose world is it? The Psalmist is clear. '*The earth is the Lord's and everything in it.*' We're able to use it. In Genesis we're given the responsibility to care for it – like a lovely garden – but it isn't ours in the sense that we are ultimately its owners, able to do with it simply as we choose. We are a generation of human beings – and by 'we' I mean every soul on earth: for whatever else it is, talk about the earth is a global issue – who unlike any generation before us has the amount of knowledge and evidence that our treatment of this world has dramatic consequences.

Experts argue whether global warming is predominantly caused by greenhouse gasses – with the vast majority sure it is. I've heard people in cold climates say that they'd welcome a warmer world. 'If Blackpool is going to be like the Mediterranean was twenty years ago, bring it on,' they say! But if you live in Oceania, in some of the Pacific Islands, the rise in temperature and the diminishing of the ice caps mean the rise in sea level is having a devastating effect, and in a few short years, some of the lowest lying islands will disappear for good, and whole cultures and civilisations will disappear. As one Fijian leader said of this impending plight, 'We will become refugees with no chance of ever returning home.'

Or take the issue of pollution. The way in which the by-products of this or that process which does something that we want easiest and cheapest, has a devastating effect on our eco-systems. Chemicals in water. Plastic reefs in the seas. Upsets to the biological balances, and so on.

Now to be sure not everybody believes that 'the earth is the Lord's', because they don't believe in God. 'This world is ours,' they say. But many then go on to say, 'though that doesn't mean we can do what we like. We've a responsibility for our planet.' And they're as critical of those who seem to think it unimportant to care for the earth as any Christian who believes that the earth is the Lord's. You see, when it comes to the health of this planet, and the issues relating to how we're to live together on it, many Christians and followers of other faiths – and many who have no religious faith at all – find themselves in much the same place. Indeed, we'll all know people who aren't Christian believers, but are more zealous about conservation and issues of sustainability, more enthusiastic and committed to recycling, more choosy about what they will buy and won't buy, more diligent about considering various environmental issues, and generally living their lives in ways that takes seriously the key issues facing this planet, than many Christians. As someone said to me recently. 'You don't have to believe in God to believe that looking after the very ground under your feet and the air you're breathing is absolutely vital.'

Christians and non-Christians alike then agree together on some very important things and use different language to describe their beliefs: 'We've failed to live in a way that's sustainable' – Christians might use the word 'sinned'. 'We need to dramatically change our way of living' – Christians might use the word 'repent.' 'We can't continue to live just how we want as if there were no consequences' – Christians might use the phrase 'under conviction.' 'The future of our children and grandchildren is more important than our own future' – Christians might say we are 'seeking salvation.' So human beings may disagree whether the earth is the Lord's or not. But in many respects it's a moot point, because very many Christians and non-Christians alike recognise that the same realities face us all, and that our future together is death or life.

Indeed, it's often people who aren't convinced Christians that point out very significant parts of the Genesis story we read today. Christians are prone to point out the sin of Adam and Eve, and talk of the fallenness of the world. Whereas it's often those who wouldn't claim to be Christian who point out that God instructs humans to tend the garden. Christians are prone to explain the significance of the serpent, often as a means of explaining why there's so much wrong in the world. But it's often people who wouldn't say they're followers of Christ who point out that there are limits. 'You can do this, but you can't do that,' they say, and then seek to apply these limits in the complex worlds of science, technology, medicine and the like.

Of all the occasions in the Christian calendar then, Harvest is a time for a bit of Christian humility. A recognition that God's intentions and priorities are sometimes better known and responded to by those who wouldn't count themselves people of Christian faith – and yet in this respect, so often think and act 'Christianly.'

The relationship of Christians with the natural world is actually a complex one. We readily affirm the beauty of the world and sing 'How Great Thou Art' with gusto. We stand awestruck on hillsides looking at fabulous panoramas. We are wowed by Attenborough-type programmes about the natural world, deeply concerned about their often doom-laden prognoses, and then as much and as easily as anyone else, live as if everything was ours to do with as we want. Indeed, some Christians are less than averagely good at caring for God's planet, because – to put it crudely – they're not worldly enough. They don't place enough importance on this world. After all, they say, 'This world is not my home. I'm just passing through.' And as a result some of us are not as committed to the stewardship of the world as others who don't believe that God created it, or that God gave humankind the responsibilities of stewardship and instructed that they tend the garden.

You see, for Christians the conviction that *'the earth is the Lord's'* isn't made simply because we believe God created it, but also because we believe that Jesus Christ, the Son of God, died to redeem it. The New Testament writers repeatedly remind us that Christ is not simply the Lord of the Church but Christ of the world. *'God so loved the world that he gave his only Son, that whoever believes in him shall not perish but have everlasting life.'* We instinctively relate that fabulous gospel passage to individuals – God loves you and you and you – and that's right. But it also means 'all of this, everything.' The 'second Adam' came – to use a phrase of St. Paul – to redeem it all, to give hope for the future, and to show us how to live. And that has as much to do with how we live on this fragile wonderful planet as any other aspect of human life.

So today, at Harvest festival, in a world facing issues that threaten us all, I ask you not simply 'Whose is this world?' but also 'Whose are you?' St. Paul, writing to the Corinthians, a group who more than many in the ancient world, enjoyed life, and did largely what they wanted with no thought for anyone else, reminded the Christians there, 'You were bought at a price. You are not your own.'

There's an old story of a church in Berlin, bombed in the Second World War. Their statue of Jesus was damaged with his hands and lower arms broken off. After the war the sculptor offered to refashion Jesus' hands. The church thought about this for some time then said, 'Thank you, but no. In a world like it is at this time we need to be reminded that – in the words of St. Theresa – "Christ has no hands but our hands."'

On this Harvest festival what does it mean to take seriously the notions that 'we are not our own,' and the 'world is not ours to do what we want with' today? In terms of our actions? Our lifestyles? Our volunteering? Our giving? Our protesting? Our loving and caring? If we believe it all belongs to God, and that we belong to God in Christ, then how shall we live together, today, here, on this fragile, polluted, endangered garden planet?

How we live out our responses to such crucial questions over the next days and weeks and years will be the best witness to whether or not we understand the nature of today's Harvest festival. Amen.

# 15

# ASSURANCE, NOT INSURANCE

The second of three Wesley or Aldersgate Sunday sermons in this collection. Even in this post-denominational age I've always thought it important, at least once a year, to preach on some aspect of the Wesleyan tradition of Christian faith. I wrote and preached this sermon during the time a good friend was diagnosed with a terminal illness and swiftly died.

Readings: John 20:24-31 & 1 John 5:1-5 & 13.

I recently heard of a person who cancelled his own life insurance policy because it suddenly dawned on him he would never receive any benefit while he was alive and couldn't receive it after he died! Which is one reason why some companies are known as assurance companies.

Today I want to talk about assurance rather than insurance, and I want you to note the end verses of our two Bible readings, both from the writings of John. In the gospel we read, '*These things have been written that you might believe.*' Then in 1 John it says, '*I write these things to you who do believe in the name of the Son of God, so that you may know that you have eternal life.*' Believing and knowing. Faith and the assurance of faith.

Assurance is a very Wesleyan doctrine, and it lies at the heart of that most quoted passage from the *The Journal of John Wesley* on 24 May 1738. How he went to a meeting in Aldersgate Street, heard the Word of God expounded and wrote, 'I felt my heart strangely warmed. I felt I did trust in Christ, Christ alone for salvation; *and an assurance was given me* that He had taken away my sins, even mine, and saved me from the law of sin and death.' So real and significant was this experience of assurance that he made it an expected, even required religious experience for Methodists. Almost as important as salvation itself was that you believed – *knew* – you were saved. You were *assured* of it.

Only after many years did John and Charles Wesley accept that God didn't appear to give such assurance to everyone, including some who were undoubtedly saved, and over time the doctrine of assurance was tempered, though not abandoned. To this day when we recite the 'Four ALLs of Methodism' it includes assurance of salvation:

- All need to be saved (the doctrine of universal sin)
- All can be saved (the doctrine of universal grace)
- All can know they are saved (the doctrine of assurance)
- All can be saved to the uttermost (the doctrine of perfecting love).

I wonder how you respond to being told you can – and should – expect to have assurance about your salvation and eternal destiny. Perhaps if we don't feel such assurance, we feel deficient, or ashamed. Perhaps if we do feel such assurance, we feel thankful or proud. Both responses misunderstand the nature of assurance. Because, like all God's blessings, assurance is a gift. John doesn't speak about assurance as something to be striven for and pursued, but as a promise to be received with gratitude. We can know.

Why is this important? Because it's good to know certain things. It's good to know your loved ones love you, and to be assured of their love. We sometimes hear people say, 'I don't think my husband (or wife, or partner, or mother, or father, or son, or daughter) loves me anymore.' 'How do you know?' we say, 'Don't they tell you?' 'Oh they say they do, sometimes, but there's no commitment, no kindness, no demonstration of love anymore.'

Now, God knows it's important and good that we know we are saved and loved, and demonstrates that in several ways. I mention three.

First, I want you to note that all through history God is the initiator of saving acts of love and invitations to a loving relationship. To Abraham God says something staggering: 'If I don't keep my covenant with you, may it be with me as it is with these dead sacrifices.' Moses encounters God in a burning bush, Isaiah in the Temple. God takes the initiative. And God takes the initiative about assurance. 'You can know,' God declares, 'that I created you, that I love you, and through the death of Jesus Christ my Son, I have saved you.'

David Livingstone, the great 19th century Christian missionary to Africa wrote in his Bible – in typical Victorian style, 'It is the word of a gentleman of the most strict and sacred honour, so there's the end of it.' We know that if a trustworthy person promises us something we find it easier to trust and believe it will come to be. How much more we should trust God's promises to us! Our wonderful God, who repeatedly demonstrates covenantal saving love to us, who assures us to believe in it and be assured of it!

Second, look at the ministry of Jesus. We often forget that the disciples of Jesus were a bunch of ordinary working folk. Straight talking, not easily impressed. Blokes who could witness something wonderful and say, 'Well, its OK, I suppose.' But as Jews they were monotheists – believers in One God. They saw Jesus when he was 'up' and 'down,' adored and despised, tired and energised, healing the sick and standing against demons, when things went right and went wrong. They saw him in public and in private. They were with him when the crowds arrived and when they went away.

And one day Jesus asks them, 'Who do people say I am?' Peter's famous response, 'You are the Christ, the Son of the Living God,' draws a gasp from some who heard him say it. For these hard-working men who became disciples, the titles normally given to Jesus – Rabbi, Teacher, Healer – had become inadequate. Their experience was that he was indeed Messiah, the Son of God. A group of Jewish monotheists suggested that God has a Son – God in two Persons as it were. And in this fragile faith they continue to travel with him, to Jerusalem. They live through the Last Supper, his betrayal, arrest, trial and beatings. They despise themselves that they forsake him at his crucifixion. They witness his resurrection – and at first can hardly believe it. They slowly come to realise that his death was the greatest act of divine love the world has ever seen, and his resurrection as God's powerful demonstration that he is who he said he is. So that one of them, John, can write after many years, 'I write these things to you *who do believe* in the name of the Son of God, so that you may know that you have eternal life.' Believe the testimony! Be assured of its truth.

Third, we have the witness of the Holy Spirit. It's the Spirit of God living in us who enables us to cry 'Abba. Father!' It's the Spirit of God who witnesses to our spirit that – yes – we are children of God. It's the Spirit of God in us who makes effective the work of Christ. And the evidence is not just 'internal.' Because every time someone recognises something of God in you, some gift or fruit of the Holy Spirit, some example of grace, some act of mercy, it is a witness that the Spirit does live in you. You can believe and know, know and believe it's true.

God, Father, Son and Holy Spirit, all bear testimony of divine love, and salvation – we can trust in it and be assured of it – even though we might not always feel it. We don't always feel the love of loved ones, but that doesn't alter the truth. We don't always live in circumstances where to feel an assurance of saving faith is easy. Feelings are, after all, fickle things.

A Christian minister and long-time family friend was recently diagnosed with terminal cancer. He died last weekend, bless him: from diagnosis to physical death in seven weeks. Helen and I went to visit him and his wife and we all knew it was to say goodbye. He was in a terrible state of inexorable decline. If ever there was reason to doubt or lose faith in God's love and power to keep, it was in such circumstances. During our long farewell conversation, which was not easy for either of us, he told me that he felt sometimes that the devil was sitting on his shoulder, whispering to him that he wasn't worthy, that he wasn't saved, that he wasn't going to heaven. 'What do you do?' I asked him, readying myself to move into 'pastor' mode. 'I tell the devil he is a liar and to clear off,' – he said – though he used much stronger language than that!

He was right, of course. Beyond all self-doubt, beyond all the accusations of the evil one is the truth. And it's this. When Jesus Christ says, 'Whoever comes to me will be saved,' then they will! Including you! And we can trust in that and know it to be true, even in times of deepest trial.

Assurance is not insurance. Assurance is loving trust in God – Father, Son and Holy Spirit – who loves us with an everlasting, saving love, and who says to each of you, today, 'You can trust me forever, and ever, and always. And you can live – and die – knowing it to be true.' Amen.

# 16

# SURRENDER! LIVING MARTYRDOM

A sermon preached early in a new calendar year and in the context of the renewal of our covenant with God using the Methodist covenant service – a liturgical jewel in the Methodist crown.

Readings: Romans 6:1-11 & Luke 9:23-27.

'*So you also must consider yourselves dead to sin and alive to God in Christ Jesus*.' So writes Paul to the Romans.

Ever since I learned that my mother's family came from County Cork, and consequently that I'm a small-part Irish, I've developed an interest in – and love of – Celtic Christianity and Celtic Christian saints. Some of those who have written and talked of Celtic Christianity and its models of discipleship and mission have intriguingly and attractively talked of it in terms of colours. They've talked of *red*, *white and green* martyrdom.

*Red martyrdom* was, of course, the spilling of blood unto death for Christ, for the sake of the gospel. Such discipleship was regarded the ultimate demonstration of faith and commitment. It was Tertullian, that great North African Christian leader who said, in the face of persecution, 'The blood of the martyrs is the seed of the Church.' Christian Celts agreed that red martyrdom was the highest calling of a Christian. But they had a problem. A problem you might find slightly absurd but which was real to them. It was this:

*Dead tree, living flowers. H. Atkins*

how do you become a martyr if nobody's trying to kill you! For they, like most of us – though not all Christians by any means: there were more Christian martyrs in the 20th century than the 2nd – lived at a time when red martyrdom was relatively rare.

So they reflected on this conundrum. Some considered killing themselves, but the idea was quickly dismissed as ridiculous as everyone knew that committing suicide wasn't martyrdom. Some considered inciting other people to kill them, but really they knew that encouraging people to break one of the Ten Commandments and thereby commit a mortal sin couldn't possibly be a God-idea. Believe me – wacky theology existed a long time before your house group started meeting!

So it was that over time Celtic Christians began to talk of different ways to live a serious Christian life, to give all to God, which today some writers refer to as 'white' and 'green martyrdom' – or in other words, deciding to live as if they were 'dead to sin and alive to God in Jesus Christ.'

*White martyrdom* is the call to live holy lives. In the words of the book of Hebrews, to remove all the sins that cling and hinder, and run the race. In some ways what hinders deeper discipleship of Christ changes over time, but in the end it's all much the same. In essence, it is all and always about three things: the world, the flesh and the devil.

It is suggested that up to one third of adults today – which includes Christian adults of course – have at least one thing in their life that's out of control at any point in time. Rather than them controlling it – whatever 'it' may be – it controls them. We may be slaves to consumerism or spending. Or have a love of possessions that exceeds what's right for followers of One who had nowhere to lay his head. Or perhaps it's our need for financial stability and wellbeing that goes far beyond what's necessary for a person who puts their faith in Christ. Some of us are addicted to habits we say we can 'break any time we want,' but seem unable to do so. Perhaps vices such as gambling, drugs, alcohol, tobacco, sex, pornography – whatever holds you back from living as if you were 'dead to sin and alive to God in Jesus Christ.'

White martyrdom took seeking the grace and power God offered to overcome such things and the belief that God wanted to deliver them from such things seriously.

Which leads us to another thing about white martyrdom, which was its focus on being filled with the Word of God, letting it steep deep within you. This was a means of holiness. In what was for a long time an oral society – meaning one where tradition and truth were passed on by word of mouth rather than by writing books – it's salutary to realise that Celtic monks knew by heart at least Psalms and the four gospels, and often the whole of the New Testament.

I remember the time when Terry Waite, the envoy of the Archbishop of Canterbury, was released after being a hostage in Beirut for almost five years. It was 1991 and he arrived back in the UK by plane, slimmer and greyer, as a large crowd of reporters gathered round, rapidly firing questions to him. One reporter asked, 'Terry, how did you survive?' and part of his reply was amazing and probably not what the reporter expected. 'I read the Office of Morning and Evening Prayer each day,' he said. Nobody picked it up at the time, but it became clear when reading his book about his captivity, *Taken on Trust*, that for most of his period as a hostage Terry Waite wasn't allowed any

103

reading material. How then did he read the Daily Office? The answer is that he knew it. By heart. More than simple repetition, he'd put that liturgy inside him so that when all seemed dark the light of prayer and the presence of God remained – alive to God in Jesus Christ.

What about *green martyrdom*? Well, if white martyrdom was about the call to holiness, green martyrdom was about the cost of obeying God's call and following Christ. It wasn't about choosing where to go and what to do; it was about being called by God, to go to this place, and do this thing. So, surrendering to the will of God, these Irish Celtic Christians left their beautiful island, and set off to wherever, sometimes not knowing where the destination lay, not knowing who they would meet, just knowing that God had called. In doing so they left behind the places and kith and kin they loved, probably weeping as they went – but going, because God had called. The nature of green martyrdom is found in the Methodist Covenant prayer. 'I am no longer my own but yours. Put me to what you will... let me have all things... put me to doing, put me to suffering... let me have all things, let me have nothing...' Dead to sin and alive to God in Jesus Christ.

The common factor, whether red, white or green martyrdom is being described, is *surrender*. Surrender to God's will, to Christ's command, to the leading of the Holy Spirit.

Somewhat late in this sermon I want to confess to you that I have a few problems with surrender. Its connotations, I mean. You see, surrender can be enforced, and often is. A mighty orc leads the armies of Mordor in the final part of Tolkien's *Lord of the Rings*. 'Surrender now,' he spits at the faithful heroes of Middle Earth, 'Surrender and we'll kill you quickly.' A mighty malicious warrior calls for the unconditional surrender of his hated enemies. Yet they despise everything he stands for. So surrender can mean, 'We don't want to, but what else can we do?' And although there's some spiritual resonance with the 'We can do no other' feeling when God calls you, the *nature* of God who calls for our surrender is absolutely crucial.

Whenever the Christian God calls us, answering the call is liberty and victory, not despair, or resignation, or defeat. You *find* your life even as you loose hold of it. The Christian God is one who knew you before you were born; who provided this wonderful world in which to live; who responded to our sin and rejection and rebellion with a plan for our salvation. A God who came in Jesus Christ and lives and loves and teaches and preaches and heals and forgives and promises and challenges. Who is betrayed and arrested, mis-tried and mistreated, beaten and tortured and ridiculed, and finally executed, praying for the forgiveness of those who crucify him. Who is raised from the grave, defeating the power of death and invites his friends to believe and follow, who promises eternal life and a final end to suffering and tears. A God who, just when we think we're left like orphans, comes as Holy Spirit, breathes into and through the people of God and says, 'Follow me... to the ends of the earth,' and whispers, 'and I am with you always, even to the ends of the earth.'

This God who demands our surrender is no tyrant orc! But this One True God does demand surrender. You ask what God requires and he always gives the same answer – not less than everything. But with such a wonderful God, a God of infinite love and mercy and forgiveness, the key question is not, 'Will you surrender?' but 'Why wouldn't you surrender?' Remember the old hymn? 'Higher than the highest heaven, deeper than the deepest sea, Lord, your *love* at last has conquered; grant me now my spirit's longing: all of you and none of me!'

Our great grandparents in faith, the Christians of the early Methodist movement, didn't talk much about surrender – perhaps because of some of its connotations we've noted – but they did talk about *yieldedness*. This is a better notion for me, for it makes more clear that there is, ultimately, a choice. To say 'I yield' implies a voluntary action not always contained in surrendering.

Remember the Covenant Prayer? 'I freely and wholehearted *yield* all things to you… And now, glorious and blessed God… you are mine, and – listen to this, it's wonderful – 'I am yours.'

So yieldedness. Yieldedness about what? Yieldedness about whatever it is that is hampering God's work of grace in you. Whatever is slowing you down in your following of Jesus. Praise God, many of us here have accepted and received Jesus Christ as our Saviour. Some of us can chart the exact time and place we first did that, others can't, but just as surely as you fall asleep in a car in one place and wake up in another, you know you made the journey. And we thought we had given him all. We sang, 'All for Jesus!' Then, over time, we realised that we had in fact given the life we knew *at that time.* And God, gently wooing, began to say to us, 'But what about this aspect of your life, and that?' And we discovered that this Christian discipleship thing isn't completed yet. That the process of living martyrdom, of holiness, of costliness, of yieldedness to God, must continue.

So today, in this season of covenant making and keeping, I invite you to choose anew to consider yourselves dead to sin and alive to God in Jesus Christ, living martyrs and witnesses of a loving Saviour. Amen.

# 17

# RE-MEMBERING

A second sermon preached on Remembrance Sunday.

Readings: John 15:12-17, Colossians 1:15-23 & Isaiah 49:14-16.

On this special day of Remembrance, and here in Westminster right at the heart of the national Act of Remembrance at the Cenotaph, I want to reflect on remembering.

First, we're required to remember the past. Today we rightly remember all those human lives caught up and laid down through wars of various kinds in various places at various times: some decades ago and some going on right now. For some of us that remembrance is deeply personal. We can recall friends, faces and people we knew. Some can recall relatives. Loved ones who went away to war and never came back, and life was never quite the same ever again. Some today will remember spouses, children and parents currently in war zones, and pray for their safety.

When *Titanic* was in the cinemas and Leonardo de Caprio and Kate Winslet were doing their stuff, a colleague told me that he'd been to see it and had been in tears throughout. I asked why and he explained how his grandfather, a trumpeter in a band, was thrilled to have been offered work by the White Star Line to serve on its new ship, Titanic. Then just three days before the maiden voyage he contracted scarlet fever and was left behind. 'When I was watching the film,' my colleague said, 'it suddenly struck me that had he not got ill I would never have existed!

For others of us the proper remembrance of a day like today is powerful, but less personal. We try to get our minds round figures like sixty million people dead in World War Two, struggling in the same way we do when we try to imagine a hundred billion stars in our Milky Way. It just blows our mind. But we do recognise the brutality of humans to one another. We do see what's going on in the world today, and we can resolve to be – as far as it lies with us – people of peace. Our remembering becomes a deep commitment to reject the ways of war and violence; to take seriously that hard but wonderful command of the Lord Jesus when he told us to love one another and that there was no greater sacrifice than that we lay down our lives for our friends. Which is, of course, exactly what he himself did, on a cross, which for Christians is understood and known to be the greatest act of love the world has ever seen.

Second, we can remember loved ones. Although this is Remembrance Sunday, it's set in the period of the Christian year known as All Saints' Tide, a season that began on All Saints Day, when we remembered the great saints of the faith. Then, the day after, 2 November, we celebrated All Souls Day – when we remembered those folk who have been instrumental in our own lives, particularly in the realm of shaping our faith and hope. So, it's entirely right to remember loved ones today. I've been moved by the way so many in this multicultural congregation mark the anniversaries of loved ones who have died. Remembering to remember loved ones is a good thing. I myself can bring to mind and remember loved ones today – as no doubt you can.

I think particularly today of my late father-in-law, Bruce. A vigorous, active, gentle man for most of his life, with a superb hymn-singing voice – he'd have loved to have been in our choir, and the choir would have loved to have had him among the baritones! But tragically, for many years before his death he couldn't remember all sorts of things. He had Alzheimer's disease, that awful condition that strips people of their ability to remember, so that they forget things they long to remember, even, eventually, forgetting those who they love and those who love them most, with the profound distress that causes to everyone. If ever we needed to be reminded of the significance of remembering, we have only to witness the slow decline of someone with this neurological disorder and related forms of dementia.

You see, remembering is part of what it is to be 'us.' Our memory is our coherence, our meaning. That's why the very word 're-member' means to put the pieces together again, in a way or shape or form where they make sense – to make a recognised picture.

The reading from Colossians offers this magnificent image of Christ as the source of all coherence and meaning. He is the recognisable picture of the invisible God, '*For in him all the fullness of God was pleased to dwell.*' In other words, when we forget what God is like – Jesus reminds us. '*In him all things hold together…*' that passage continues. For Jesus Christ is the meaning, the coherence of everything that is. And through him, '*God was pleased to reconcile to himself all things, making peace through his blood on the cross.*' You see, Christ is the supreme re-memberer, bringing together things on earth and heaven.

Psychologists tell us that our remembrances are of two kinds: there's what's called the *semantic* memory, which is our memory of facts, or complex actions, like riding a bike, driving a car or playing the organ. Then there's the *autobiographical* memory where we're able to reconstruct happenings from our own lives in considerable sensory detail. When we remember such occasion, it's like we can re-live it, we're back there, with the sights and sounds and smells of our remembrance. How wonderful are our brains that we're capable of that kind of remembering! Our memories aren't like DVDs, inserted and played when we want to recall the past. Nor can memories be taken out of one person's head and placed in another – like Professor Dumbledore does in the Harry Potter films. These memories are ours, and they make us what and who we are. So today we remember loved ones – living and departed – and we give thanks for them.

So… remember the past… remember loved ones… and thirdly, remember what God has done for us. Why? Because so many of us have a kind of spiritual amnesia. We forget so quickly. Remember the people of Israel wandering in the desert. They're rescued from slavery – and they forget. They're led through the Red Sea – and they forget. They're rescued from those seeking to destroy them – and they forget. They're led into the Promised Land – and they forget. They're provided with food – manna and quails – and they forget. They're declared to be God's people and given the Law - and they forget. And before you know it they're erecting idols and worshipping them! 'What has God ever done for us?' they say. It's like the Monty Python sketch in *The Life of Brian*: 'What have the Romans ever done for us?' Implying 'nothing at all,' but ending up with a list of good things as long as your arm. The scene concludes with John Cleese saying exasperatedly, 'Yes, well, apart from sanitation, medicine, education, wine, public order, roads, fresh water systems, and public health… What have the Romans ever done for us?'

Are we like that with God? How often God brings us through trials, answers prayer, blesses us, guides and protects us, and within a couple of days it's all forgotten – what has God ever done for us? Well, God has known us before we were born, loved us with an everlasting love, given himself in Jesus, on the cross, raised him to heaven where he prays for us, Jesus who will return one day for us – so that we might be where he is – forever. God who sends the Holy Spirit to be our courage, guide, comforter and helper. That's what God has done for us. So don't forget to remember. Because as Remembrance Sunday reminds us, without reminders we tend to forget even the most significant things in our lives.

We're told that of all our faculties, hearing is the most durable.

That's why, when people are in coma, loved ones are encouraged to speak and read to them. That's why when people are dying, speaking peaceably to them is good. Voice is important.

Fourth and last, then, I want you to remember *that God remembers.* Those you hold dear in your memories – God remembers. Those who we see no longer – God holds. When Bruce, my father-in-law, finally died, a Methodist minister whose own mother had died from the same form of dementia wrote to us. 'We may forget God,' she said, 'but God never forgets us. We may come to forget who we are – but God does not forget. We may no longer know God – but God always knows us. We may even come to fail to recognise our loved ones – but God never fails to love and know us. We may no longer be able to speak – but God speaks gently to us.' Remember the passage we read from Isaiah? '*Zion said, "The Lord has forgotten me." Can a woman forget her nursing child… Even these may forget, yet I will not forget you. See, I have inscribed you on the palms of my hands…*'

Peace. No more suffering, says the Voice. The most important Voice. The Voice which, at the end, is the most important Voice of all. For at the end of all our remembering – and our forgetting – is the hope of heaven, offered by the One who holds all things together. One who will not forget any of us. Amen.

# 18

# GIVE GOD WHAT'S RIGHT, NOT WHAT'S LEFT

A sermon on giving.

Readings: 2 Corinthians 9:3-11 & Mark 10:17-27.

The reading from 2 Corinthians is one of several in the New Testament that refers to Christian congregations collecting gifts of money for believers in need in other places. Indeed, it's one of the recurrent themes of the New Testament that disciples of Christ are called to be generous in terms of sharing what they have and who they are. In this instance Paul writes that he's sending some believers to the Christians in Corinth to collect a 'bountiful gift' that they've clearly promised to give. It's for 'the saints' – the

*Money and coffee. M. Atkins*

fellow believers – in Macedonia. Fellow believers who, in an age without tablets, smartphones and Skype, they would never have met. Today, I want to use this passage to note various things about giving, about stewardship, about generosity, about seeking to be good disciples of Jesus Christ. To work out how better to give God what's right rather than what's left.

I want you to note first that the money gift is in response to need. Human need remains a key driver of generous giving. Just think of the huge sums raised for those affected by natural disasters or personal tragedies. God seems to have hardwired humans in such a way that, at their best, they're instinctively moved to give when faced with need and trauma. There is, placed deep within us, a need to give to those things which are right. That's why many of us give in several directions, not just one. We support a number of good causes rather than simply 'the Church.' Giles Fraser asks a key question: 'For whom is my money good news?' And if the answer is, 'Well, just ourselves really,' then as disciples of Jesus we have serious problems.

Sadly, but understandably, some people are deeply suspicious of giving to Christian ministries. We've all heard of spiritual conmen, greedy TV evangelists and powerful pastors with expensive, extravagant lifestyles! All of which fuels the belief of some that the Church is just selfish and self-serving, building bigger and bigger barns while preaching that that's just what you shouldn't do. And that's sad, because in the vast majority of cases it's simply not the case. It's far more the case that when we give, whether by cash, contactless card payment, direct debit or envelopes, we take an active part in a community that seeks to resource God's kingdom, to partner God in the transformation of the world – 'on earth as it is in heaven' – as we pray each service. Through our gifts, we support people in underdeveloped countries and resource the local foodbank, house the homeless and enable some stunning youth work in the local estates. Through our gifts we enable our children and young people to be taught and nurtured among others in a caring and godly context. We release resources to bless the downhearted, visit the poorly, offer benevolent gifts as needs arise, and provide a space and place where people can meet with others to mutual benefit and friendship. When we give, like the Corinthian Christians of old, we're giving to the *ministry* of Christ, not just meeting the budget we've set ourselves. Nor do I mention these things to puff us up with pride – 'Hey, aren't we good?' – because giving to the ministry of Christ is right and proper, and Christ demands and deserves our generosity.

No wonder then, second, that the generous giving of money is regarded by Paul as a good indicator of how *serious* we are about our discipleship. 'Put your money where your mouth is,' he effectively tells the Corinthians, otherwise your promise to give will be an empty boast. That in essence is what the story of the rich young ruler is about. 'You say you want to be my disciple,' asks Jesus, 'How serious are you?' 'Oh, very serious,' the rich young man replies. 'I've done all the right religious things and I believe all the right religious things.' 'Marvellous!' says Jesus, 'Just one more thing then. Go give away all you have, then come and follow me.' And the rich young man can't.

Make no mistake, money is the sacrament of seriousness. To quote Giles Fraser again: 'God only knows you're serious when he's got your wallet!' You see, when we make our offering it's as if we were standing on the offering plate. That's one reason why we stand when we bring the offering forward. Not because we respect money itself. But because we are saying, 'This is mine, but it's really yours anyway, because everything I have is yours. And because I'm yours, I place myself before you, again, anew. Use these gifts for the good purposes of your kingdom, and use me for those same purposes.' How serious are we about following Jesus Christ? Jesus, over half of whose parables were about how we use the possessions and resources we have.

Then, third, notice that there's an issue of *timing* in relation to giving. Paul sends some folk to Corinth to collect the offering because time is of the essence. 'Get it ready,' he says. 'I'm telling you we're coming so we won't find you unready, else both you and we will be humiliated.' To give at the right time is really important. Let's use an important and quite common example.

Most of us still work on the basis of hoarding. We don't like calling it that, but that's what it is. In other words, we keep what we have, saying that when we die, others – family, friends or causes – will get the benefit, receive the inheritance. But often that's too late. In fact, it's arguable that it's not *given* as much as *left* – after all, we keep telling each other, 'You can't take it with you!' For those of us who have them, take our children or grandchildren as an example. God willing, when we die at an old age, we hope our children will themselves by then not need our money quite as much as now, when they're still paying mortgages and raising families. In very many cases the time to help our children and grandchildren is when they're younger and have greater need of money. They'll actually benefit from it, and we can receive their thanks instead of wondering if they are quietly hoping we pop our clogs in the not too distant future!

One preacher made this very point and some weeks later received a letter from a young couple she didn't know, thanking her for the sermon. The wife's parents had attended the church, heard the sermon, gone home after worship and sent her and her brother cheques for £5,000. 'Please preach more sermons on stewardship,' the wife wrote, 'especially when my parents are there!'

Fourth, the text makes it clear that giving must be *voluntary*. Look at verse 7. '*Each of you must give… not reluctantly, or under compulsion, for God loves a cheerful giver.*' In other words, the attitude with which we give is critically important. So let me say very clearly, if you are giving reluctantly, don't give. Pray, and ask the Lord to get you to a point where you can give gladly, and then give gladly. Similarly, if you feel you're under compulsion to give. Or again, it's quite possible to make generous monetary gifts which effectively try to buy God's favour. Though if we imagine that God doesn't know when we're trying to haggle or strike a deal, we're really silly! It's possible to give a small amount which represents much – like the widow's mite. Some of us have much and God knows that. Some of us have little and God knows that too. But whether a lot or a little, the attitude with which we give is crucial.

If we're honest with ourselves, lots of us were once more passionately committed than we are now. We gave our lives to the Lord, and then in subtle ways, over the years, we've taken it back. Bit by bit. 'I said you could have my money Lord – but that was when I didn't have any!' 'I said you could have all my life Lord – but that was before I got this new job… or met this new special person.' And God says, 'At what point did you take back what you gave to me? At what point did you begin to act as if what you have and are, is yours? At what point did you cease to offer what's right and offer what's left?'

I remember Donald English preaching at *Easter People* shortly after the death of his beloved wife, Bertha. He'd been given the theme, 'Be Good.' His hearers probably thought he'd ignored the theme as he told stories of God's goodness, and bore testimony to God's faithful keeping, even through his recent bereavement. Then, as he closed he said, 'So I don't ask you to be good. Rather I ask you, with such a forgiving, loving, caring God, why *wouldn't* you be good?' Ultimately disciples want to do what pleases the one they love, the one to whom they owe the deepest unpayable debt. Yet – wonderfully – a debt to One who doesn't make you feel a debtor, but invites you to be a member in the family.

When we reflect about giving, the same motive applies. Why wouldn't we give, to one who loves us and gives himself completely for us? '*The person who sows sparingly, reaps sparingly,*' says Paul. '*And the person who sows bountifully will reap bountifully. Let each one think what they might give.*'

Lastly, I want you to note that the outcome of this thoughtful, cheerful giving to the causes of God's kingdom is that we can rely on God for provision, which is abundant, and the *satisfaction* of having shared in good work. In short, the giver is enriched. Now we all know there's lots of teaching about giving which tends too easily towards the notion that you give in order to get more. Or that God will so reward you that you will never be out of pocket. Note, then, that the word Paul uses here is 'enriched' – and means you are given things of value. True riches. So, in terms of stewardship, when we encourage 'enoughness,' encouraging each other to get out of debt, to refrain from extravagant luxuries we don't really need, to avoid wasting money, to be generous with our children and grandchildren, to learn contentment with less, we are talking about enrichment. When we resolve to live as wise stewards, it honours God, it relieves stress, it builds self-confidence, it removes guilt, it increases our ability to witness to God's goodness, it enables us to give ever more generously. In a word – our life is enriched.

A Christian died and was being shown around heaven. As the angel showed him round, he noted the finery and splendour of some of the rooms and spaces. But when he got to his own room, it was poor by comparison with bare floors and cheap furniture. The man was shocked and said to the angel, 'How come those people were in such fine places and all I've got is this?' 'Yes, I'm sorry,' replied the angel. 'This is all we could do with what you sent us.'

Jesus said, '*Where your treasure is, there your heart will be also.*' Jesus made it clear there's a close tie between people's purses and their hearts. He didn't say, 'If a person's heart is right, they'll give.' He said, 'When you invest your money in something, your heart will follow.' So when we give, we're helping to put our hearts in the right place. I think that's what Paul is getting at, rather than notions that God wants us all to possess more and more money. Enriched lives and enriched living is the promise of God to those who dare to give cheerfully and generously.

And at the last, when we're stood before the throne of God, recognising like never before that, in fact, we *couldn't* take any of it with us, will we wish we'd put more treasure in heaven? And if that's the case, what are we going to do about that now, before we get there? Today, choose to give God what is right, not just what's left. Amen.

# 19

# DIGGING YOUR OWN WELLS

A weakness of my preaching is made clear in this collection – I don't often preach from the Old Testament! And even then, I usually focus on a particular phrase or verse. Here is one such sermon. It was preached when in a congregation comprising over thirty ethnicities – London is a global city and MCHW reflects that – many members of African heritage were celebrating their education, a number being schooled in distinguished Methodist and Christian schools throughout West Africa.

Readings: Genesis 26:12-18 & John 4:7-26.

*'And Isaac dug again the wells of water which had been dug in the days of Abraham his father…'* (Genesis 26:18)

For all his fame we don't know much about Isaac. God is often referred to as the God of Abraham, Isaac and Jacob – which is a neat way of referring to God who is beyond naming – but there isn't exactly a comprehensive biography of Isaac found in the Scriptures. Some of what we know comes through this passage in Genesis. Isaac is nomadic, probably living in tents – possibly fine tents – and moving from place to place, most likely following the seasons for water and food for his livestock. He's a wealthy man, and the land he moves around on is probably his own, inherited from his father.

Indeed, as the son of the great Abraham he has inherited all sorts of things. A prestigious name, lots of land, an extended family including servants, herds of animals, sources of wealth creation. He was probably well educated by the standards of the day. He has it all – he is the 'rich young ruler' of the Old Testament. Except for one thing. He has to dig the wells his father dug again in order to find water – a gift of life.

*Well digging in Uganda. M. Atkins*

You see, inheritances are good, but there are some things you can inherit and some things you can't. There are some things that can be done for you, and some things you must do for yourself. And working out which is which is vitally important to every one of us.

In spite of being two thousand years old, Christianity is only one lifetime from extinction. It has lasted two millennia because in each and every generation people have come to believe in Jesus Christ and take their place in his family on earth – his One Holy Church. If everyone ceased to do this, then we are the last generations of Christ's disciples, Christ's Church. As Billy Graham used to remind his hearers, 'God has no grandchildren, only children.'

This is a source of worry to many of us. Parents concerned about the Christian faith – or lack of it – in their children and grandchildren. Friends are concerned about their friends. That's why it's right to bear witness, carefully and sensitively to our loved ones and friends, to pray for them, to model good, attractive, real, fragile but honest Christianity as we live out our lives.

# DIGGING YOUR OWN WELLS

When I became a Christian as a teenager, quite a number of my friends chose to become followers of Christ too. One went home and said to his Christian mother, 'Mum, I've become a Christian. Why didn't you tell me to do it years ago?' I don't know if she tried to reply, but I do hope she gave him a hug and expressed her joy at his decision.

Another of the young people my age, who'd been in the local church I joined for many years and had attended Sunday school from being very small (when most of us hadn't), came up with a classic. 'I'm already a Christian, my dad's an elder!' When, after her own conversion to Christ, she'd say, 'I used to think I was a Christian because I was raised in the church and my parents were Christians. But I had to make the decision for myself. I came to see that you can't live on someone else's faith.'

There are few better examples of this than John Wesley himself, a key earthly founder of Methodism. Raised in a profoundly Christian home, by a great and godly woman and a devout ordained man, schooled in a church school and attending a Christian university, he – with brother Charles – sets off to Georgia in America to be a missionary there. It was a disaster, and he returned home a couple of years later, depressed and dispirited. He wrote, 'I went to America to convert the Indians, but O who shall convert me?' That time of searching later resulted in his experience of May 1738 when he talks of his heart being strangely warmed. 'I felt I did trust in Christ, Christ alone for salvation,' he wrote, 'and an assurance was given me that he had taken my sins, even mine, and saved me from the law of sin and death.' But the opening words of this event in his journal are just as important to us today. 'I went very unwillingly to a society in Aldersgate Street,' he writes, 'where one was reading from Luther's preface to the Romans.'

I want you to notice a couple of things: first, inheritance is very important. Wesley, hearing Luther as it were, dug his own wells that night. Isaac dug again the wells of his father Abraham. About the girl I spoke of, many years later when we met, we were talking about those good times, and I reminded her of what I've just told you. She said, 'I agree with what I said. But I think I see now that I was able to say "Yes" to following Jesus, and to quickly know what I was doing when I did that, because my dad and my mum were good people of faith, and I loved and admired them.' That education you received. Those of us who had godly and loving parents. The experiences which have shaped you to be the person you are: your character, your morality, your lifestyle. Thank God for it all and for all who gave you the inheritance you have.

Second, know that inheritance itself isn't enough. Isaac inherited the wells, but he couldn't get the life-giving water they supplied until they were re-dug. Wesley heard Luther's account of faith in Christ, but had to open his own heart and permit God to warm and fill it.

But, third, I want you to notice too that when Isaac did dig out his father's well, he too found water. It wasn't dried up. Living water wasn't missing. When Wesley, encouraged by the words of Luther opened his heart to Christ, Jesus drew near to him too, and filled his life and heart.

Do you remember the old song? 'It is no secret, what God can do. What he's done for others, he'll do for you, with arms wide open he'll pardon you; it is no secret what God can do.' Well it's true. Jesus says to each of us, 'I am the living water. Whoever comes and drinks of me a spring shall spring up in them which is eternal life.' It's no secret. The well isn't hidden. Or dry. But you have to drink from it yourself.

So, finally, notice that it is only when Isaac has dug out the wells of his father and drunk the water that God's promise to his father Abraham is given to him. *'Fear not, I will be with YOU, and will bless YOU and multiply YOUR descendants.'* And it is only from this time that the writers of the Old Testament begin to refer to God as 'the God of Abraham AND Isaac.'

So, on a day when we give thanks for our inheritance, particularly of education, but also of many more things, we must ask ourselves some searching questions. Have we used our inheritance well? Has it produced in us the proper works of service, humility, kindness and goodness? And have we made this inherited faith our own? Have we dug the wells ourselves and sought and found the living water that will be found there? When we do that, and keep doing that, we will understand better the nature and purpose of our inheritance – what it is and what it isn't. Amen.

# 20

# DISCIPLESHIP – METHODIST STYLE

A third and last Aldersgate Sunday sermon in this collection. There is at MCHW a genuine interest in and desire for Methodist and Wesleyan theology and thinking. So much so that I was asked on arrival to preach regularly so that the whole congregation was better able to live as Christian disciples in the broad and rich Methodist and Wesleyan tradition.

Readings: Philippians 1:3-10 & Acts 2:38-47.

When we say discipleship Methodist style – what do we mean? We don't mean that Methodists believe fundamentally different things than all other Christians. Indeed, Methodism is just common, brilliant, wonderful, basic Christianity – ordinary, awesome orthodoxy. John Wesley talked about Methodists as those who sought to return to primitive Christianity, by which he meant the passion and purity of faith he believed was found in the early Church as witnessed by the New Testament.

But like all Christian traditions, Methodists have certain themes and moods and tones that make it what it is, and I want to talk about some of these this morning.

First, Methodist discipleship has an evangelical spirit. We Methodists believe that Jesus came, lived, died, and rose again, and that he offers salvation to all. That there's not a soul on this earth who is beyond the reach of the love and saving power of God. Therefore, ALL can be saved. John Wesley went the length and breadth of this land many times, over a long ministry, and if there is one repeated theme in his lifelong work, it's the phrase, 'I offered them Christ.' Offering Christ is at the heart of Methodism still, and lies at the heart of Methodist church life. If the life of a Methodist church isn't about offering Christ, in word and deed, through grace and goodness, it isn't, in the fullest sense, a 'Methodist' church. Offering Christ is in our Methodist blood. It's one of the reasons Methodism was raised up by God. And what you're 'raised up by God for' is very important.

If we asked our Baptist brothers and sisters in Christ about their origins, they could tell a torrid tale of persecution and ostracism. A story of conviction that, among other tenets of faith and practice, the sacrament of baptism is reserved for those who can consciously and personally affirm faith in Jesus Christ. If we asked our Reformed brothers and sisters in Christ about their origins, they could tell of a radicality of faith that often marginalised them in the societies in which they grew – a story of conviction that, among other tenets of faith and practice, the role and relationship of the minister and the autonomy of the congregation were key.

When you ask about the origins of Methodism, the story is not one fundamentally about theological convictions, about sacraments or about the nature of ministry or the congregation, leading to particular practices or structures – though in time such issues would help shape Methodism. Methodist origins lie in proclaiming Christ, overtly and often publicly, and particularly to those who did not know him as the loving Saviour and Lord of all, or attend church.

Now – and this is important – I don't make this point to suggest that Methodists are better or worse than other denominations. All Christian traditions have riches that they bring to the table, and together we are the One Church of Jesus Christ. I make the point to draw attention to a particular theme that gives Methodism its mood and tone, the theme of evangelical Christianity.

That term 'evangelical' is sadly debased today for many people. It's often associated with hard, bigoted, right-wing, ethically and politically shaped Christians, an implied Christianity that many find unattractive rather than attractive, more callous than Christlike. Today, evangelicals are sometimes portrayed as against everything and for nothing. So it's very important to make clear that when I say Methodism possesses an evangelical spirit, I do not mean in the sense of hard, insensitive, arrogant evangelism, but rather in terms of a gentle, attractive invitational offer of the gospel, by people who remind you of the Jesus they love and follow and talk about.

I've told you of a time when, at Easter People, I'd been preaching at the event earlier that evening and now sat in the hotel lounge, and got talking to the preacher from the night before, a nice man, an American from one of the Baptist denominations in the United States. We were talking about the event we were at and I congratulated him on his very good preaching the night before. Then he said, a little left field, 'You Methodists really want people to get to heaven, don't you?' I was taken aback, and said, a bit bemused, 'Yes, don't all Christians?' 'I guess so,' he replied. 'But my church seems to spend more time telling people what it's like in hell rather than urging them to get to heaven.'

Now I've no idea whether his assertion about his church is true or not, but I've often thought about that impromptu conversation. In terms of Methodism he was on to something. At our best we Methodists want everyone to become the best human being they can be – especially in terms of deepened discipleship of Christ, greater likeness of Christ – what John Wesley called Christian perfection – discipleship that's evident and worked out in every area of our lives.

The second theme is an emphasis on a 'big' Holy Spirit. What do I mean? Well, the Holy Spirit is often experienced as the emboldener, giving courage and strength to Christian believers, and Methodists readily believe and bear witness to that. The Holy Spirit is often experienced as the comforter, giving hope in times of trouble, and Methodists gratefully believe that and know its truth. The Holy Spirit produces fruits in Christian disciples – love, joy, peace, gentleness, kindness, and so on… and Methodists cherish these as necessary for Christian discipleship and holiness. The Holy Spirit also bestows gifts: words of knowledge, wisdom, the gift of prophecy, faith and healing, working miracles, discerning spirits, tongues and the interpretation of tongues – gifts given by the Spirit for the common good, given to some for the sake of others. And although Methodists aren't Pentecostals in the sense of belonging to that Christian tradition – though nowadays many Methodists around the world, particularly in South America, are 'Pentecostal' in their worship and spirituality – Methodists gladly experience these charismatic gifts of God's Spirit.

But what I want you to note is that all this wonderful ministry of the Holy Spirit – emboldening and comforting, producing fruits and giving gifts – are all works in Christian believers, are all blessings to the Church.

To explain what I mean by a 'big' Holy Spirit we have to note that in addition to all these blessings, Methodists also emphasise the work of the Holy Spirit in the world. A Holy Spirit without barriers or borders. The Holy Spirit is the 'Go-between God,' active in the space between heaven and earth, present in everything God has made, convicting, convincing, rescuing, restoring and revealing the loving nature of God in a needy world. The Holy Spirit is also the 'Go-before God,' at work, alive and abroad in people and places everywhere.

When I worked at Cliff College, the students used to go on 'mission.' They'd go in small groups, by invitation of local churches, to live, work and witness for a couple of weeks in localities all over the UK. Shortly before setting off they'd gather in the college chapel with a member of staff to pray and talk about the mission ahead. I'd often ask a team, 'Why are you going on mission?' Various responses were offered, but usually, in and amongst the comments was something like, 'We're going to take the gospel to the people there, to introduce them to Christ, to invite them to receive him and be filled with the Holy Spirit.'

Some days later, shortly after the students had returned to college and descended on the shower and laundry rooms like locusts, we met again in the chapel for a debrief. I'd ask them, 'You said you were going to take Christ to the people there. How did it go? What happened?' The response was always the same: 'Jesus was already there.' 'So what did you do?' I'd press. The response – in different ways – was always the same: 'We tried to work out what God was doing and just joined in.' It was a very 'Methodist' piece of learning!

A Holy Spirit there before we are! In a situation before we are. Alive in hearts before Christ is known. A 'big' understanding of a 'big' holy Spirit is a very Methodist approach and such an important understanding of the Spirit today.

*John Wesley statue, Savannah, GA. H. Atkins*

Third, Methodists emphasise a 'catholic spirit.' What do we mean? A catholic spirit can be described as open-handedness. A generosity of spirit. A humility about ourselves and a willingness to work with others, to see good in others.

The notion of the catholic spirit is often connected to John Wesley. In 1755 he preached, wrote and published a sermon by that name. In it Wesley outlined the essentials of Christian experience, and his resolve to work with all those who honoured Christ

131

and promoted Christ's kingdom, even if he differed from them in some doctrinal matters. Earlier he had published another sermon along similar lines, *A Caution Against Bigotry*. In both sermons John Wesley spelt out his warning against the sectarian spirit that divides the people of God and prevents Christians from understanding that God is present and working in fellowships, parties and denominations other than their own.

His sermon on the catholic spirit was based on an obscure Old Testament passage in 2 Kings, where Jehu questions Jehonadab. 'Is your heart right, as my heart is with your heart?' And Jehonadab answered, 'It is. If it be, give me your hand.' Wesley urges that this example was one that every Christian disciple should imitate. Jehu's question is not about Jehonadab's opinions but about his spirit, his attitude and his affections. How does he regard his neighbour? In a word, is there love in his heart? Wesley pleads that even allowing our differences of opinions – our 'contrary convictions,' to use a phrase common to British Methodism today – we must not let this stand in the way of mutual Christian affection. 'Though we can't think alike, may we not love alike?' he asks. Christians have differing types of public worship, differing ideas about church government and ordained ministry, differing practices about the subjects and mode of baptism, and much else. Yet far more important than any of these is the question: do you love God and all humankind?

With the world as it is at present, can there be a more significant call to Christian disciples than to adopt and live out the catholic spirit?

Disciples are followers. Followers of Jesus. To be a disciple of Christ in the Methodist, Wesleyan spirit and tradition, is to live out discipleship in an evangelical spirit, experiencing and accompanying a 'big' Holy Spirit, and being profoundly shaped in character by a catholic spirit. Such disciples remind us of Christ. Such discipleship is really good, good news for the world today, and I urge you to it. Today. Here. Now. Amen.

# THE CHRISTIAN YEAR

# 21

# WATCH. PRAY. STAND.

The first of two Advent sermons. This one particularly focusing on the final return of Christ rather than, as Advent progresses, on preparation for the coming of the Christ-child at Bethlehem.

Readings: Jeremiah 33:14-16 & Luke 21:25-36.

Advent is here. Surely in recent decades the most messed about Christian season of them all! From October, tinsel and trees appear, and Christmas ditties play incessantly in supermarkets, effectively squeezing out the Christian season of Advent with its focus on prayerful self-assessment and preparation for the coming of Christ.

The word Advent means 'arrival' – particularly the arrival of Jesus Christ, of course. But not just the arrival of the baby of Bethlehem – Mary's child – but also Christ who will come again: for Jesus is our future as well as our past. So today we focus on Christ's final return, noting that we cannot know quite when it will occur, but must watch and pray and be ready for his coming.

The return of Jesus Christ as Lord – sometimes known as the 'second coming' – belongs to a broad doctrine of Christianity known as eschatology, which is the study of the end times, the last things, and has given rise to some of the most variegated beliefs in Christianity. Drawing on a number of passages in the Scriptures, not least the last book of the Bible – Revelation – Christians have tried to work out how references to martyrs of the faith reigning with Christ for a 1,000 years, evil being poured out on the earth, a final judgement being passed, and the promise, 'Surely I am coming soon,' relate to each other. Accordingly, quite different expectations about the end times and the return of Christ have come about.

Some suggest that Jesus will physically return to earth, followed by a thousand years of peace – a golden age, before taking his own to heaven. After which disaster strikes the earth. For those who like long technical terms, this is known as premillennialism.

Others look at it the other way around. There will be a millennia of peace, where Christianity flourishes, *after* which Jesus will return, take his own to be with him, *followed* by the awful period of evil talked about in Revelation taking place. This view is known as postmillennialism.

Then there are those who reject the idea of a literal thousand-year-long physical reign on earth, suggesting that Jesus Christ is presently reigning through his Church. When it's pointed out that it is over 2,000 years since the first Christian Pentecost, it's explained that a millennium-long reign is simply a metaphor for 'a very long time,' but that there will be at some point a final judgement and an everlasting reign. This is known as realised millennialism.

The passage in Luke we read today tells of the turmoil on the earth prior to the coming of the Son of Man. The day of his arrival nobody knows. And when you've been alerted for the umpteenth time by someone claiming to know when Jesus will return (it's next March, Thursday, the 2nd, at 5.34pm precisely!), it's good to remember that Jesus repeatedly said that no one knows the hour of his coming.

But if we're unsure of the time of his coming, we can be sure of at least two things.

First, there will be an end, a time when God says 'Enough!' and those things that we think so permanent – and act and live as if it will be like this forevermore – will pass away. This world, with its heady mixture of love and beauty, hate and violence, isn't the final word. For the Christian believer, 'this' is not how it all ends or where it all ends. And some things that presently seem to make no sense will make sense, like someone had turned a tapestry around and we see the picture, when previously all we saw was randomness and loose ends.

Second, we're instructed to be ready. Jesus doesn't foretell of 'signs' in the expectation that nobody will notice or recognise them, though it's clear many people won't. Rather he says, '*When you see these signs, know this, the kingdom of heaven is near,*' your redemption is at hand. So what is important is to be ready *whenever* Jesus comes, and the reading suggests that a state of readiness requires us to watch, and pray and stand.

Watch. Following a series of terrible terrorist attacks, including one only yards from this building, there follows a period of the highest level of alert. But as the days and weeks go by it's realised that this is unsustainable: we can't be on the highest level of alert, with things closed down and cancelled, and many staying indoors, all the time. Sooner or later things have to return to some sort of normality, even if the threat of an attack remains.

So what does it mean to 'watch'? It doesn't mean to be obsessed with trying to second-guess each happening. And it probably doesn't mean living every aspect and every moment of life as if the end would come about in half an hour. That isn't sustainable, and living in fear is not what God desires.

I think it means to be watchful. Be watchful for that which leads to Jesus. The wise men usually come at the end of the Christmas story. But they're only there, in Bethlehem, after Christ's birth, because they're watching and waiting and studying weeks and months before. Be watchful, too, for that which pleases Jesus. Some follow a pattern of prayer at the end of each day by reviewing it and offering it to God. How have I served God? What do I need to remember – and forget? Of what do I need to repent? In this way we're watchful about our own lives. Are we being the kind of person who lives out a life that demonstrates we are watchful for the coming of Jesus Christ?

Pray. I suggest we're to be prayerful rather than seeking to 'pray' all the time. By all means pray, overtly, regularly, faithfully, diligently. Alone. Together. But also *live* prayerfully, so each breath and action is an offering to God. Watching and praying are needed to sustain a state in which whenever Jesus comes, we're ready, in that we're living lives that please and honour our King.

*Sculpture at La Sagrada Familia. H. Atkins*

Watch, pray... and stand. In an apocalyptic situation, with the world appearing to come apart, its foundations shaking, most people duck and head for cover. Yet, says Luke, this is precisely the time for people to show courage and faith. In a time of hopelessness, stand for hope. In a time of violence, stand as peacemakers. In a time of oppression, stand for justice. Stand for what's right.

To 'not know the hour' can create a kind of 'Well, what does it matter?' mentality. 'I don't know when Jesus will return, so I won't bother about it. I mean, what's the point? He'll come when he comes!' I'm suggesting this morning that though we don't know the hour, it really *does* matter how we live, and act, and pray, and serve, and worship. That is like the women in Jesus' parable; the lights are ready to be lit, and we are ready for his coming. And a thing of potential dread becomes a thing of faithful anticipation.

Advent expects the arrival of both a judge and a saviour. You stand before a judge to receive the sentence, but in this case the one who pronounces the sentence is also the one who pardons it, and we're left standing in awe, before a loved one who has set us free.

In Advent I always pose myself a question, and I share it with you. What if Jesus returned before Christmas? How ready are we for his coming? If you knew that today was the day, would you be comfortable with that? What would you change about your life, even at this late stage? Before the coming Christ-child rightly takes the centre stage – these are proper questions for disciples, during Advent. Amen.

# 22

# WHAT WE KNOW AND WHAT WE DON'T

*Advent Sunday.*

**Readings: Isaiah 2:1-5 & Matthew 24:36-44.**

I wonder how many read the sermon title for today and remembered that famous statement of Donald Rumsfeld. 'There are known knowns,' he said. 'These are things we know that we know. And there are known unknowns. That is to say there are things that we know we don't know. But there are also unknown unknowns. These are things we don't know we don't know.'

Somewhat ironically, given that his statement was made in the context of the Gulf War, Rumsfeld draws heavily on an Arabic proverb which goes like this:

> He that knows not, and knows not that he knows not is a fool. Shun him.
> He that knows not, and knows that he knows not is a pupil. Teach him.
> He that knows, and knows not that he knows is asleep. Wake him.
> He that knows, and knows that he knows is a teacher. Follow him.

Today the Christian season of Advent begins, a time when we think of preparing for Christ's coming: coming not only as a human baby in a stable in Bethlehem, but as the Risen One who states he will return as Lord and King and Judge of all. I want us to reflect on what it might mean to be ready for either – or both – events.

So, what do we know and what do we not?

Jesus is coming again – we know that. Christians can faithfully believe that just as surely as there was a time when God created the earth, just as surely as there was a time when humans messed

it all up, just as surely as Jesus Christ God's Son walked this earth, just as surely as he lived and died and was raised to life again, so he will come again.

What we don't know is exactly when. It's at a time we do not know.

Which means that

*Old rope. H. Atkins*

those who tell you they do know should be regarded with a great deal of scepticism. If even the Son of God doesn't know – as the text in Matthew suggests – why should we believe that a shopkeeper in Seattle or a preacher in Paris might know?

In the days before mobile phones I lived in Devon with my wife Helen and our then small boys. Our parents used to call us up and tell us they were coming for a visit. Since they lived in North Yorkshire and often stopped in various places along the way, and the motorways were unpredictable, we were expecting them but weren't sure when they would actually arrive. 'We'll see you when we see you,' was a favourite phrase of my father-in-law. The certainty of their coming but ignorance of the precise time of arrival motivated us being ready. Get the beds made and room ready for whenever they arrive. Cook something that won't spoil.

But there are signs to watch for, indicators, hints. Note the ordinariness of the signs in these verses from Matthew 24: people are working, talking, eating and drinking, and so on. Just like any day. But, note, the signs in the earlier verses of Matthew 24 talk of wars, famines and earthquakes as signs to look out for. So, will Christ be coming when there are wars and rumours of wars? Yes! Will it be suddenly, like a thief in the night of which there is no sign or warning? Yes! It's Matthew's way of saying that we don't know when Christ will come. But we're asked to be ready whenever it may be.

Now what does it mean to be 'ready'? I suggest it's by being about the things that we know Jesus wants us to be about. Doing the things of the kingdom. Partnering in the mission of God. Being agents of peace and justice. Living as servants of the Servant Jesus. Being where we should be, doing the things we should do, being the people we should be. We're told by experts that children who receive a smile by those collecting them from school are more settled and healthy than those greeted with a frown or anger. Therefore, being ready, being faithful, is to live in such a way that when he comes, Jesus will smile rather than frown. So we know he's coming but we don't know when.

Second, we know there will be a judgement. Christ's coming will be the day of judgement. We know it will be an end to things as they are. It will be God's 'Enough!' We sometimes fall into the trap of thinking that because everything is roughly like it always has been for as long as everyone can remember, it always will be that way. It takes larger swathes of time to realise the profound nature of change in the world. In fact, there's no guarantee that the world as we know it will continue to be as it is. Indeed, if you were a betting person you'd bet that it won't.

Not only do we know that there will be a judgement, we know the extent of the judgement, who it will include. He will come again to judge the living and the dead, the creed says. Judgement includes all who are living, and all those who have ever lived –

143

in short, everyone! Some say Christians won't be judged, but the Scriptures don't suggest that. Rather they suggest that Christians are subject to judgement, but that the penalty of judgement – the sentence if you like – is paid for by Christ. Billy Graham used to tell a story of receiving a fine for speeding. He went to court, pleaded guilty, and the local judge fined him. Then, out of respect for the young evangelist, he paid the fine himself. That's something like the judgement of Christians. God pronounces sentence then in Christ, pays it, with his own life, on the cross. As an old Good Friday hymn goes, 'On the cross condemned he stood, sealed my pardon with his blood.'

So we know there will be a judgement and we know its universal extent. What we don't know is the exact nature of the judgement. Those graphic medieval pictures of hell, with demons and red devils with fiery tridents, with beasts roasting humans on spits, are assumptions, graphic guesses arising from theological convictions. I'm not saying hell is nice! I am saying that just as we don't know exactly when Christ will return, so also we don't know the exact nature of the judgement. Nor do we know when this judgement will be, any more than we know when Christ will return.

In *The Chronicles of Narnia* by C.S. Lewis, in the final book called *The Last Battle*, Aslan – the Christ Lion – returns as king and judge. The nature of judgement is based on who can look Aslan in the face as they pass by. Those who look away and cannot hold his face, go left to the darkness and those who know him and look into his face with love go right into the light.

Or again, there's an old story told by Herodotus. A philosopher from Athens comes to Sardis and meets the great king of Lydia, Croesus, who has legendary wealth and power. Croesus shows the philosopher around proudly, then asks, 'Who is the happiest person you have seen?' expecting to hear of his own blessedness. Instead, the philosopher surprises him by telling him of a man called Tellus, whom Croesus has never heard of. Tellus lived in a prosperous city, had five children, lived to see his grandchildren, died a brave death and received a public funeral. Croesus couldn't understand the story. 'Why is Tellus more blessed than I?' he asks. The philosopher replies that nobody can be truly blessed before their death, because a life still being lived is a life not yet complete, and no one knows what the future brings.

You see, it's the final outcome of things that determines the meaning of everything that goes before it. Look to the end!

So, this Advent we remember, mercifully, that there is still time, time to amend our lives. There is this morning, now, an opportunity, to turn away from all that denies God to turn again towards Christ, to resolve afresh to live in such a way that when he comes again, for all the impending certain judgement, we can look him in the face – and rejoice.

Third, and the last thing we know we can know, is this: that there will be a new heaven and a new earth. Judgement is not the end. Even death is not the end. For all its emphasis on judgement, the Christian Church down the ages has looked upon the return of Jesus Christ as 'the Blessed Hope.' Alleluia!

But we don't know exactly what heaven will be like any more than we know exactly what hell will be like. What we do know is that the Lord Jesus will be with those who love him, and forever. 'I will come again,' says Jesus, in John's gospel, 'and take you to be with me, so that where I am you shall be too.'

In another of C.S. Lewis's books, *The Great Divorce*, Lewis tells a story of heaven and hell, both visited by a bus trip! At a certain point in the book the character being shown around heaven by his Scottish guide sees a figure, radiant and beautiful. 'Is that, is that?' he says, looking at the figure, imagining that it might even be the Lord himself. His guide looks at the figure, and realises what the man is thinking. 'Ach no,' he says. 'That's someone ye'll have never heard of, her name is Sarah Smith and she comes from Golder's Green.' Because in heaven even the least of the Lord's followers will be radiant.

So what do we know and not know? That Jesus Christ will return – but we don't know when. That he is the judge of all – but we don't know the exact nature of the judgement. That the promise of heaven awaits those who love him. So we do what all sensible folk do. Be ready. Are you ready? If not, there's time, but we don't know how much. So best be ready now, today, don't you think? Amen.

# 23

# 'MOST HIGHLY FAVOURED LADY'

Preached in the season of Advent and at the request of members of the congregation who commented that they couldn't remember a sermon about Mary. This sermon was a modest attempt to begin to rectify the situation.

Reading: Luke 1:39-56.

'Will you be preaching about Mary? I don't think I've heard many sermons about Mary.' That's what some of you have said to me and I said I would gladly preach one, and this is it!

Sadly, Mary, the mother of Jesus is something of a casualty of Christian history. In some traditions, particularly – but not only – Roman Catholicism, you'll often hear sermons about Mary, because she's regarded of crucial importance. Protestants on the other hand, dispute some of the claims made about her and so don't focus on her much at all.

For example, Roman Catholic beliefs urge us to pray to her, or more precisely to use her as an intermediary: after all, it's said, who better to get the ear of Jesus Christ than his mother? But Protestants reject 'praying to Mary.' 'You only pray to *God,*' they say, 'through Jesus Christ and in the power of the Holy Spirit.' Then there's the 19th century Catholic doctrine of the Immaculate Conception: the belief that from the moment of her conception by the Holy Spirit Mary *herself* is sinless – free of original sin.  After all, it's asserted, how can the sinless Son of God be born of a sinner? To which Protestants point out that the Bible makes it clear that all – except Jesus – have sinned and fallen short of the glory of God.

And so on and so on. The more that's made of Mary by some Christians, the more wary are others, leading to the suggestion that we Protestants – and Methodists stand in the broad Protestant tradition – might have thrown the mother out with the bathwater so to speak! As one Methodist said, responded to his Protestant critics who questioned his devotion to Mary, 'Why won't you let me love her?' It's a good question.

Mary is, after all, the mother of our Saviour Jesus. She carried him in her womb, gave birth to him, nurtured and raised him to manhood. Surely among all the figures that surround Jesus, like St. Peter and St. Paul, she deserves at least as much attention, respect, admiration and love!

I want to focus on three simple but vital things this morning.

Mary makes it clear that women are used by God in the essential purposes of God. Well, a sceptic says, even God probably had to use a woman to give birth! But God uses women and not only when God has to. The Christian Church hasn't always seen this very clearly, and we live with the consequences to this day, and in many cultures. But the reality is that women are called into discipleship, called to Christian obedience, called to exercise ministry, called to lead God's people, just as men are.

Second, Mary shows us what's involved when you are obedient to the call of God.

It certainly involves *courage and faith*. Think for a moment, the fact that Mary agrees to be the mother of Jesus is just amazing! A young woman – a girl of about fourteen many think – who deals with an unexpected, life-changing, dangerous and future-threatening situation with trust and grace. It's a decision that starts her down a potentially long and difficult road when she says 'Yes' to God. But Mary did say 'Yes' to God. She trusted that God wouldn't ask something of her, and then let her down. And so she responded to the angel with words of faith: '*May it be to me as you have said.*' Having faith in God when circumstances are against you isn't easy. Obeying God's call isn't easy, it's sometimes meant to be difficult, to be hard.

Do you know that we are called to the same kind of costly, risky faith as Mary? When we step out in faith, when we respond obediently to God in the way Mary did, God is able to use us to bring about great things as well. God continually looks for faithful followers to work with and through. God continues to call people and ask them to step out in faith, and when they do, God then uses their faith to change the world.

It also involves the *audacity* to believe God's call. I love the fact that Mary believes that God has chosen her to be the mother of Jesus Christ. She hears the momentous news of the angel and says 'Yes.' She had the audacity to believe that God had chosen her to be the mother of the Messiah.

Moses and a number of other Old Testament figures tend to respond to God's call with excuses: 'I'm not good enough, God, get someone who can talk better.' Or, 'I'm too young,' or 'I'm too old,' or 'I'm not sure Lord, give me a sign,' or 'Give me five signs!' 'Prove it to me and then I'll believe it.' But Mary simply believes that God has chosen her, and because she believes it, she is able to do what God had chosen her to do.

And just as God chose Mary, ordinary lowly Mary, God also chooses ordinary folk like you and me. Even today. God doesn't ask anyone to do exactly what Mary did – that happens once, for all – but like Mary we are called to be God's servants. Not because of our abilities, but because God is gracious. God has chosen to use your life in God's mission for the world. God has chosen you and me to be the loving presence of Jesus Christ.

Finally, I want you to note that *Mary loved Jesus all her life*. In fact, Mary was the only human being with Jesus throughout his whole earthly life.

She was the only person to love Jesus before he was born – so many mothers-to-be become aware of how much they grow to love their unborn children. They know and love him or her long before birth.

Mary loved Jesus at his birth, as she wrapped him carefully in swaddling cloths, fed him, changed him and laid him down in the manger. Mary is sometimes referred to as the 'womb of God.' It's not my favourite description of her! I know it refers to the fact that this young, poor, ordinary but extraordinary woman is chosen by God to bear the Son of God, and that's recognised as a great honour and privilege. I know that in ancient days, when our knowledge of how biology works was much more basic than it is now, it was commonly thought that the male supplied everything necessary for a baby to grow. A woman's womb was regarded simply as an incubator to enable that which is purely the creation of the male to grow. But you know, there's so much more to Mary than a womb!

Mary loved Jesus *as he became a young child.* His childhood was Mary's focus. Mary was nurturer, not simply incubator. A parent. She with others had the key role in the growth and maturing of the person who was always by nature God's Son, but who as truly human still needed washing, and feeding, and clothing, and educating, (and perhaps teaching right from wrong) and encouraging (and perhaps reproving).

Mary did a great job! Remember the comment when Jesus is in the temple aged twelve, and amazes the temple priests with his profound wisdom: 'Is this not Mary's son?' And Mary is so proud, like a parent at a graduation service, even as she ponders, wondering what this all means. At a very practical level, Jesus Christ who began his earthly ministry is a testimony to her parenting, alongside Joseph and others in the close circles of ancient communities.

So Mary loved Jesus before his birth, at his birth, as he was raised. And Mary loved Jesus when they were together at the *wedding in Cana,* Jesus' first miracle recorded in John. When you read that gospel story, you almost sense that Mary was urging Jesus to perform a miracle that he wasn't fully ready for. She can perhaps be excused for wanting him to meet a need, show what he can do – lots of mothers do that!

Mary even loved Jesus when he told the crowds that she and her other children weren't his true family but that those who did the will of God were his true family. She could've been very hurt, but she understood. And she stood by.

Mary loved Jesus *at the foot of the cross*, as she suffered the unbearable pain of watching her child be executed and could do nothing about it. And her heart breaks.

Mary loved Jesus when he *was raised from the dead* and appears to his followers – the Risen Christ. And she loves him as *he ascends to heaven*, and she never sees him again – at least on earth!

Make no mistake, God chose well when he chose this humble, obedient young woman. There's so much to admire in her example and faith, so much to seek to aspire to in our own lives.

Mary loved Jesus all his life, from before he was born until the day she died, and even after. And Jesus loves us all our lives, from before we were born until the end of the earth. The Son of God who died on a cross for the sins of the world is also Mary's Son.

How can we best respond to such love – the love of Jesus and the faithful love of his mother? We can choose, like her, to love him with what life we have left. And if we choose to love him with what life we have left on earth, that's marvellous. But just as marvellous is that this relationship of love doesn't end at our earthly death, but extends beyond it and lasts for eternity. Those who choose to love Jesus Christ, and follow him, even today, do the right and best thing. And we can do that right thing right now, right here, for the first time or once again. Amen.

# 24

# THE GOD WHO IS CLOSER

One of our largest congregations each year is the evening Carol Service, run in partnership with Premier (Christian Radio). Some two thousand people, led by a large choir and orchestra sing traditional carols and hear the familiar lessons of the Christmas story. The service is recorded, mixed down and broadcast on Christmas Day. The preacher has around ten minutes to speak (as if it were Christmas Day) to both the congregation and the many thousands of listeners to the broadcast some days later.

Since the beginning of time human beings have believed in gods – small 'g'. The gods they believed in lived far, far away, out of reach, lords of the heavens. If they communicated with hu-

*Carol Service at MCHW. D. Forshaw*

mans at all, it was at a distance, perhaps through the movement of a star – which is one reason why wise men seeking the birth of one born king of the Jews looked up for one. But for the most part the gods were not only distant but also disinterested in the affairs of the earth and its largely insignificant inhabitants.

So that if you were interested in these gods, you had to seek them out. Perhaps through secret knowledge or words. Or you'd bribe them through offerings to make themselves known or to act in some way. Though in truth the last thing most gods wanted was to be known by the likes of us! They were, after all, above and beyond it all.

Yet despite this, humans created gods of all sorts of things. There were gods of the weather and the seasons, of fertility and barrenness, of health and wealth, of protection and danger, of life and death, mostly everything really. No surprise then that the Roman and Greek cultures dominating the world at the time of Jesus' birth had hundreds of gods for dozens of situations, to whom prayers were made and gifts offered. Anything to catch their attention, to come out of hiding, to get them on your side. The ancient gods had this in common. They were distant and disinterested.

It was the One True God – God with a capital 'G' – God the Father, Son and Holy Spirit, who broke the mould of the distant, disinterested god. This One True God wasn't created by humans but instead created them and placed them in a beautiful world and told them to flourish. Nor was this God disinterested. Because when God's loved and lovely humans rebelled almost before the paint of paradise was dry, God was devastated. Other, lesser gods would've just walked away and left us to it! But this God didn't. Instead of hiding away, this God sent prophets and messengers, symbols and signs, law and love, urging silly, sinful humankind to come back home.

And time and time again we rejected God's invitation of life, choosing our own pitiful, violent, selfish ways instead.

Then this One True God did something truly wonderful. 'If they won't listen to my prophets or obey my laws,' God said, 'I'll go to them myself. I'll show them how to live. And I'll pay the price that forgives their sins myself, in blood.' And God made flesh, God with skin on, Jesus Christ, God's holy and only Son, came among us. Born to one of us, born as one of us.

Those we called gods were disinterested in humanity: this true God lays his life down for us. Those gods needed seeking out: this true God comes to seek us. Those we called gods were distant. This One True God came close. And he still does.

Some years ago a friend of mine wrote a book called *Finding Faith Today*. It arose from several hundred interviews with folk who'd recently come to a living Christian faith. Some used the language of conversion, some the language of journey. Some marked their faith by baptism, some by confession. In reflecting on these many testimonies the key ways how people today find faith became clearer.

Some of the factors were unsurprising. For instance, very few of us respond positively to the gospel of Christ the first time we hear it. Most of us come to say 'Yes' to Jesus Christ because, many times, over time, those we like and love and respect show us love and care, and gently and clearly invite us to follow Jesus. And pray that we do – until we do.

But some of the factors were more surprising, particularly the responses to the question, 'What have you learned about God since you came to faith?' Because there was one very dominant response. It was this. 'Before I came to faith I thought God was unknowable, distant and remote, unfeeling, that God wasn't bothered about me. Now I know that God loves me, is close to me, and is real to me, and that's changed my life.'

*'And you shall call his name Emmanuel, which means God is with us.'* We've read it just now. God who comes close. That's what's happening in the stable at Bethlehem, in the life and death and resurrection of the Holy One born there, and ever since, right down to this very special Christmas Day.

You see, if God is closer than we think, then we don't have to travel very far to find God. God wants to be found. In a stable, by shepherds and wise people, yes, for sure. But also by you and me, today, now. We who are healthy and sick, vital and tired, contented and questioning, cynical and open. Those of us with sins and crosses in our lives – because he went to one to redeem us, and offer hope and life. To all of us. Each of us. Every one of us. Including those who we love, and are concerned for, and so want them to experience the nearness, the closeness of God in their lives today.

Christianity. What is it? The Greeks made it into a philosophy. The Romans made it into an institution. The Middle Ages made it into an empire. The Enlightenment made it into a culture. The Church tries to make it into an organisation, and the West makes it a disposable hobby, a pastime.

But in the end Christianity is a relationship, a relationship with Jesus Christ, the Son of God. Who loves you and offers his life for you. Today, on this Christmas Day, this special day of Emmanuel, draw still closer to the One who draws close to you. Amen.

# 25

# HE CAME

A second short sermon preached at the Carol Service recorded for Christmas Day broadcast on Premier (Christian Radio).

Different Christian traditions tend to emphasise different aspects of the life of our Lord Jesus Christ. Protestants often focus on his resurrection – Christ is risen! It's an empty cross. Alleluia! Roman Catholics often focus on Jesus' passion and crucifixion – Christ has died! It's a full cross. Alleluia! Orthodox Christians tend to emphasise his incarnation – He came! Alleluia! And they're all right! On this Christmas Day I want us to focus on Christ's incarnation. The fact that he came.

Both words are important. He *came*. And *he* came. The sheer wonder that the Son of the Living God should come to earth, to us, a race of rebel sinners, isn't lost to the writers of the New Testament. In Matthew's account of the birth of Christ we're told he's to be called 'Emmanuel,' meaning 'God with us'. He came. And in that wonderful passage that begins John's gospel we read: '*He came to his own… and the Word became flesh and dwelt among us.*' He came. That wonder is also found in the carols we sing. 'Veiled in flesh the Godhead see! Hail, the incarnate Deity! Pleased as man with men to dwell, Jesus our Immanuel.' God. With us.

It's a marvellous thing that from the moment humanity polluted paradise and rebelled against God, God sought to redeem and

*'Hands across the divide', Northern Ireland. M. Atkins*

rescue us all. God made a covenant with Abraham and Noah, gave the Law through Moses, spoke his messages through Isaiah, Jeremiah, Hosea and other prophets. But nothing worked quite as God desired it, such is the rebellion of human-kind.

So it was, in the fullness of time, that he came, one of us, living among us and teaching us how to live. Christ, God's Son came and laid down his life on a cross to save us, the holy for the unholy, the lovely for the unlovely. So that everyone who believes in him, and receives him, might be saved. He came.

Do you remember the story of the little girl frightened in a thunderstorm? 'Don't be afraid, Lucy. God will look after you,' says mum. And the thunder rolls and the little girl buries her head in her mother's breast and says, 'I know God will look after me mum. But at times like this a little girl like me needs someone with skin on.' And God knows that. And he came.

Presence – actually being with someone – is so very important, isn't it?

One of my biggest failures of love and care happened when I was eighteen and had been a Christian only a few months. Paul, my severely mentally handicapped elder brother, a resident in a secure mental hospital, went missing on the cold, bleak moors around Todmorden. I learned this as I got back from Youth Fellowship, and found my mother in tears and my father stony-faced and silent. I helped myself to supper, said goodnight and went to bed!

# HE CAME

In the morning I discovered that my parents had spent most of an anxious night awaiting news of Paul. Was he dead or alive? Missing or found? I also discovered that they'd rung our local Methodist minister who – bless him – had come round and sat with them most of the night, until at about 4.30am the hospital had rung to say that Paul had been found, cold and hungry, lost and frightened – but alive. The minister came.

No surprise then that many years later, when talking about who he wanted to take his funeral, my dad wanted that Methodist minister. 'When we needed him, he came,' he said.

Of course, Jesus' death is not the end of the story. If it was, we probably wouldn't be telling the story of his birth today. Jesus Christ was raised from death by the power of God, ascended to his native heaven and sent the Holy Spirit to be with his people forever.

You see, the one who came, *still comes*. Today. To us. To save us. To help us, to empower us, to stand with us against injustices. To reveal the things of God. To the frightened. To those who dread this time of year. To those spending Christmas without loved ones – for the first or fifty-first time. To those with much anticipated plans and those without any. To those of us who know we still need a rescuer, a saviour, a messiah, a Lord, because we're still lost.

Will you receive him? Because the gift of Jesus is always the gift of himself.

But as the story of my brother Paul, my parents, our minister, and me makes plain, there's another challenge, and that's to be an agent – a representative – of the One who came and who still comes. Years afterwards, when I was myself a Methodist minister, and Paul had sadly died, my parents and I talked about the night he went missing, when I went to bed and our minister didn't. 'What did he say to you?' I asked. 'Can't remember,' they said, 'Not sure he said much at all.'

To 'be there,' sometimes to act, most times to listen, always to be present, in his name, is crucial Christian ministry today.

So, he came – the Son of God. And that's wonderful. And he comes still – to us, to help and heal and rescue us – and that's wonderful too, and can happen even today. And he comes whenever we who are his followers go, in his name, ready and willing to be his hands, his voice and love in a needy world. Amen.

# 26

# 'CHRISTMAS' BEGINS WITH 'CHRIST'

In recent years MCHW has developed jazz services led by an excellent jazz band. Jazz Vespers takes place six times a year and near Christmas it's Jazz Carols, usually recorded for broadcast and another occasion requiring a short sermon.

*Martyn placing Jesus in the MCHW crib. (anon)*

Have you ever looked at a word you've seen thousands of times, and suddenly understood why it means what it means? You probably haven't, being much sharper than me, but I had to become a Christian in my later teens to read the word 'Christmas' and make the connection – Christ-mas... the festival, remembrance, celebration of Christ. It's obvious, but it completely escaped me for years.

Christmas in today's Britain makes clear we are a plural society, and for very many people Christmas isn't a Christian faith festival because they profess another faith. We're also what some call a post-Christian society. It's undoubtedly the case that over many centuries Christianity has shaped the practices, traditions and values of our society, but less so nowadays. No surprise then that statistics tell us the largest faith group in the country is now those who say they have no formal faith at all.

Some of these folk are quite content with our Christian heritage, without attending church much at all. I'm reminded of that wonderful one-liner by Bishop Festo Kivengere many years ago, when he visited Britain. As he boarded the plane back to his native and much troubled Uganda, he was asked, 'Bishop, what have you learned about British people?' He replied, 'I've learned that British people don't go to church, but that they do like a church not to go to!' Others are more negative about Christianity in British tradition, past and present. They want to reduce or even eradicate Christian heritage and influence from our society. It – and all formal religious faith – belongs to a former age, they say, and the sooner it's left behind the better.

Yet almost none of us would vote to abolish Christmas. There would be general uproar. For us all – of formal faiths or none – Christmas is a welcome holiday, a few days off work, or school, visiting family and friends, time to take a deep breath near the darkest time of the year.

Faced with Christmas in contemporary Britain, Christians can often be the 'bah humbug' grumpy brigade. My late, lamented friend Rob Frost used to say of Christians going to church, 'They look like they're going to the dentist… and when they come out, they look like they've been!' But as people of the greatest good news story this isn't our best role. I think there are better ways of celebrating Christmas than being grumpy or judgemental.

First is to rejoice! To join the revellers! In Jesus Christ our God comes to us! And we see his glory, full of grace and truth. Does the angel appear on the hillside and declare, 'Behold, I bring you tidings which will make you so depressed?' No! 'I bring you tidings of great joy!'

And in the form of a human baby. I have three grown, married children, and, this year, a new grandchild. What a dramatic effect a new baby has, and in the vast majority of cases, it is the source of great joy. The infant Christ's coming declares the great love God has for us all – every soul on this wonderful, fragile dangerous planet. We're not alone: *Immanuel* – God with us – is with us. Ultimately, what is there not to rejoice about?

Second, there's a challenge to us all to be people whose *lives and lips agree*. To be people of hospitality in a world where so many live without a thing called home. To be subversive people who increasingly refuse to play the unsustainable planet-wrecking game: who reject that more is never enough. People who act and live as if it was true that it is more blessed to give than to receive. People who turn the darkness off and spread light all around. People who've come to understand why 'Christmas' is spelled 'Christ-mas' – and all year round! People who know that the coming of Jesus Christ can't be packed away until next year, like our decorations, or left by dustbins like our bald Christmas trees. We know that when Jesus Christ calls people to follow him – which he does, even today – he doesn't go on to say, 'Between the twelfth of December and Twelfth Night.'

It can be tempting to spend this holy season in plural, post-Christian, commercially driven Britain, grumpy that so few appear to understand that Christmas begins with Christ. But a better way – and, incidentally, a way that millions of Christian folk around the world who live in places not much shaped by a long Christian tradition do so well – is to seek to live out their faith with joy and with their lives and lips agreeing.

Wouldn't it be fantastic if those who know followers of Jesus, even like us, found it easier – rather than harder – to believe in a loving God who can be known and trusted? Wouldn't it be marvellous if those who bump into Christians – whether in places of work or rest, in homes or churches – found it more possible to encounter the Word Made Flesh, and perhaps for the first time come to understand more fully that Christmas begins with Christ? Let's resolve and seek to be such people!

It's likely that some of you listening are realising more and more that Jesus Christ is the meaning of life. The well-loved carol we sing now includes these words: 'Where meek souls will receive him, still the dear Christ enters in.' Every one of us, for the first time or the hundred and first time, can invite Jesus Christ to come and lead and shape our lives, and know he'll do just that, and for our good. For you, Christmas can begin with Christ. Then it really will be Christmas. Amen.

# 27

# TRANSFIGURATION – LIGHT AND ENLIGHTENING

The image of drawing back curtains to let light in came from the late great Donald English, as I suspect did several turns of phrase found in this and other sermons in this collection. This sermon uses several images to explore the text both as exposition and narrative.

Readings: 2 Corinthians 3:12-4:1 & Luke 9:28-36.

This morning I woke up and the early spring sun was streaming through the curtains. It was so bright. The whole room was lit up. For a moment I thought there was a fire outside. I drew back the curtains and was almost blinded. When my eyes adjusted, it was like a film set with those enormous lights making things crystal clear.

*Light in the Pantheon, Rome. H. Atkins*

The Transfiguration of Jesus, which we're focusing on today, is one of those occasions when God draws back the curtains and says, 'Are you watching? Are you listening? It's really important you understand this.'

The New Testament Greek word used here for 'light' is the same word used for a bolt of lightning. We sometimes say, 'It hit me like a bolt of lightning!' meaning that we suddenly realise something, apprehend its meaning. The Transfiguration of Jesus is meant to have the same effect. God pulls the curtains back and Peter, James and John are meant to see and understand something significant. But not only them. All readers of this gospel story are included – we are meant to see, and hear, and realise something important, today.

Well, what are we meant to realise? The first clue is the *voice from heaven*. '*This is my beloved Son, whom I have chosen*,' God says, '*listen to him*.' Jesus, the Rabbi teacher from the backwater Galilee area is in fact God's Messiah. Who Jesus is, the person who these disciples have been with, is made clearer – like a bolt of lightning!

Another clue is that we're up a *mountain*. Mountains were often, in the ancient world, a place close to gods. In the Judeo-Christian tradition mountains were often regarded as the place where God spoke. Remember Moses on Sinai? Remember Elijah, hiding up a mountain when he hears the still small voice?

We talk of mountaintop experiences. It's true that sometimes the mist comes down and you can't see your hand in front of your face. But other times you get breathless to the top of a high place and the view, and the clarity – you can see for miles. But rarely do we stay on a mountaintop, much less live there. Most of us go up and down mountains quite quickly. Which is one reason why the building of tabernacles is not a good idea, but we'll come to that shortly.

In one sense, the lasting value of a mountaintop experience is when you aren't there. It's like remembering a lovely holiday when you're back at work. We often remember being on that high place with its clarity and vista when it's raining or dull. Spiritually, we often remember a mountaintop experience when life is hard and God seems far away. We remind ourselves, 'Remember that time when God was so real, so near,' and we take heart. When we're down and dry, it's sometimes the remembrance of being in a higher place that helps sustain us. We recall that, after all, it's the same faithful, reliable God who is with us now, just as then.

Notice too, the state of the *disciples*. Luke says they grow sleepy. How on earth you can be sleepy on such an occasion beggars belief, but they are! This may relate to their physical state; they've climbed a mountain after all. But just as likely it's a description of their spiritual state. Remember how, when Moses has received the Law from God on the top of a mountain the people to whom he returns are also spiritually sleepy? And remember another time when these three men are filled with sleep? In the garden of Gethsemane, when another great 'God moment' is underway.

I wonder if our following of Jesus is on autopilot. Did we come here this morning thinking, 'Just another day, just another service'? Are we sleepwalking in our following of Jesus? Because it's when the disciples become fully awake that they see and realise what's happening on the mountain. To be asleep when you're not meant to be is a potentially spiritually dangerous place. Wake us up, Lord! From time to time God does pull the curtain back and says, 'Do you see? Do you understand?' And if we're not awake, not ready, we miss all sorts of things that God wants to teach us. So we don't learn and we don't grow. Are you asleep or awake to God today? And if asleep, please – wake up!

The Transfiguration then, is essentially God revealing the true *divine identity* of Jesus. He's more God than the disciples think – and often we think. Just as the events in the Garden of Gethsemane are essentially about God revealing the true *humanity* of Jesus – because he's more human than the disciples think – and we often think.

Today some of us need to know and realise that Jesus is more divine than we acknowledge. The person for whom nothing is impossible. The *Lord*. Equally, there'll be some of us today who need to know and realise that Jesus is more human and more perfectly human than we appreciate. He's not far away. He's not remote. He *does* know and understand what our lives are like. You see, whatever our situation, Jesus Christ is who we truly need. Hear that today!

Then there's *Moses and Elijah*. The embodiment of the Law and the Prophets. '*I have come to fulfil the Law and the Prophets*,' says Jesus. And here they are. Moses, who goes up a mountain to receive the tablets of the Law from God and returns, his face shining, radiant because of that encounter. And as God draws the curtains back the disciples see the radiance of Jesus. They're meant to see and understand. Here's the new and greater Moses. Here's the One who reflects the glory of God.

Moses and Elijah are also figures who had peculiar exoduses. Moses gets to see the land promised to Abraham but doesn't enter it. It's assumed he dies but his body is never found. Elijah doesn't die but is taken to heaven in a fiery chariot. So here we have two figures who have 'gone before' with significant 'leavings' talking with One who will shortly have a significant leaving. It's probably not very good Christology, but I imagine these great figures of faith counselling – even encouraging – Jesus. 'It's alright to make this journey. It will be very hard, but Almighty God can be trusted.'

Then we have dear old Peter. Moses and Elijah show up and if he'd been around today he'd have got his phone out and tried to get a selfie with the group! Ever the hospitable one, he says, '*Let me build you three tents – or tabernacles – Lord.*'

There's so much wrong with this! Luke gives extra clues because the text in brackets reads, '*He did not know what he was saying*'! No surprise then, that as Peter suggests making dwellings, the sun disappears, the brightness goes, the curtains close. Some suggest that this is because Peter isn't 'seeing.' What's he not seeing? He's still not seeing who Jesus really is. Possibly he's putting Moses and Elijah on a par with Jesus, regarding them as greater than his teacher and friend or even seeing them as three equals. But, 'No' says God, '*This one is my beloved Son*.' Which is probably why, at the end of the passage we are told 'only Jesus' remains. Elijah and Moses aren't, ultimately, the point. Jesus is the point.

But there's also the problem of what building tabernacles means. They're dwellings. 'Let's stay here, Lord, on this mountain,' says Peter. 'You and Moses and Elijah. You can stay here and I'll start a new business. Tourists can come to this mountain and can take selfies with you all. It'll become a place of pilgrimage like no other on earth.' Maybe. But it would be the end of Christianity.

Some see this part of the text as resonant of the temptations of Jesus in the wilderness – which we'll look at next week as we enter Lent. In the wilderness it's the *devil* who tempts Jesus: 'If you are the Son of God…' then do this or that or the other. Here on Mount Horeb it's one of Jesus' *closest followers* that tempts Jesus in a different but similar way: 'Lord, you don't have to go to Jerusalem, stay here with these great figures of our faith, stay safe.'

As we walk through Lent we're going to repeatedly see occasions when people say to Jesus that he doesn't have to go to Jerusalem, that he mustn't be handed over to the Jewish authorities, that on no account must he suffer violence and finally be put to death. That simply can't be what God requires. So here, at the Mount of Transfiguration, the disciples urge him to stay. 'Let's preserve this moment,' they say. 'Let's put it in spiritual aspic. Let's always stay on mountaintops. Let's not go to Jerusalem.' God forgive us, some of us would say exactly the same thing in the circumstances!

But Christianity is a travelling, living faith. It doesn't really deal in those kinds of tabernacles.

There's a silly story – though I'm sure it must have happened at one time or another – of the tourist who goes into the site of Jesus' tomb outside Jerusalem. He emerges somewhat disappointed and is heard to say to his friends, 'Huh. There's nothing in there!' How we misunderstand our faith so often!

Is Christianity still a living faith for you? Are you still obedient to what God is calling you into? Or are you attempting in all sorts of ways to 'stay here' – wherever 'here' might be for you? 'Let us build a place in which we put you, Lord. So we've got you where we want you.' Rather than hear Jesus say to us, as he said to his disciples on the Mount of Transfiguration, 'We're going. Follow me.'

So let's not be sleepy. Let's not deliberately mishear. Let's not try to lock our Lord into a nice, cosy place where we want him. Let's remind ourselves again that he is Lord and we are his people. He invites us to follow him, and he chooses the route, just as Jesus ignores the disciples and sets off down the mountain, leaving them to decide whether to follow. Today is a day to place yourself next to Jesus, for your right place and path is wherever he is and wherever he goes. Amen.

# 28

# LORD OVER ALL?

A sermon preached in Lent rather than, strictly speaking, a Lenten theme. Or is it?

Reading: Philippians 3:17-4:1.

I've seen two adverts recently that use much the same imagery to make the same point. Both feature a parent and a child. In the first, the mother, sat on the sofa, drags deeply on a cigarette while watching TV. And across the room, watching the mother, is a young son, who mimics her, dragging on an – at the moment – imaginary cigarette. In the second advert the father is fishing, accompanied by his young son. The father casts a line into the water, and the son standing next to him does the same. The power of influence. Especially the power of the key influencers in our lives.

In today's passage from Philippians, in verses 17-19, the writer creates a contrast between influencers who aid us being 'in Christ' – and those who don't. Nearly all parents can discern between the two. 'I don't like you going around with that gang, they're a bad influence.' 'I do wish you'd join that group, there are some lovely kids there.'

Earlier in Philippians, Paul has made it clear that salvation is a gift flowing from God's love, effected and effective by the death of Jesus Christ on the cross. So heaven isn't a reward, but a fruit of having faith in Christ, in accepting the salvation he has brought about through his death for us all. Here in this passage, Paul warns his readers that not all lifestyles help take you to heaven. It's possible to live a life that flies in the face of the salvation Christ has offered to us. So, he says, in effect, 'Choose carefully who and what influences your life.' And he goes on to identify two ways of living which he says are 'enemies of the cross,' that is, they take you further away from heaven rather than towards it.

First is the way of living advocated by the 'Judaizers.' This group are referred to earlier in Philippians, but also in other parts of the New Testament. In Galatians they're referred to as the 'circumcision party.' This was a group of Christian believers in the early congregations of the Church who insisted that Gentiles must submit to the Law of Moses as a precondition of belonging to Christ. About this and other things they were legalists – 'You do it this way, and if you don't do it exactly like this, then it doesn't work, or count, it isn't right or pleasing to God.'

At other times in Christian history there've been those who took much the same view about certain words and actions. For example, one of the disputes relating to the Protestant Reformation in the 16th century was about the mass, the communion service. Some – mainly Catholics, but not all – said the mass, if it was to have spiritual power, if bread and wine were to become the body and blood of Christ, had to be done exactly right. This included using exactly the right words. It was referred to as *ex opere operato* – meaning quite literally 'by the words said.' It was a legalistic approach to mass, which caused many Protestants to point out that as far as they were concerned, getting the words right was less important than the spiritual state of the priest and the people receiving communion. These things are important too, replied the Catholic scholars. But, some insisted, unless it's done exactly like this, in a church like this, by an priest ordained like this, it's unworthy and spiritually useless.

# LORD OVER ALL?

A lifestyle of legalism, Paul says, is an enemy of the gospel, in that it doesn't help you receive Christ, it doesn't honour the gift of salvation, nor does it help you get to heaven.

But Paul warns of another lifestyle which is an enemy of the cross, another poor model which won't help make you a citizen of heaven. Alongside the legalists in the congregations of the early Christians there were 'antinomians,' which means 'those without laws,' those who said, 'I'm set free by Christ,' by which they meant they could do virtually whatever they pleased. They were known as the 'freedom party.' Paul may be referring to the *Gnostics*, folk who melded their existing beliefs with a professed Christian faith, and were going around saying, 'My relationship with Christ is spiritual, mystical, *and, therefore,* what I do with my body is of no consequence, no importance.' You might know people like that today!

Having identified these two groups – legalists and antinomians – those ruled by laws and those who reject them – Paul notes that they both have one key thing in common. It's this. They live their lives in a way that rejects or opposes the lordship of Jesus Christ over the whole of human life – body, mind, spirit. He's not Lord of it all.

Now in case you hadn't already noticed, there are legalists and antinomians in the Church today! Including us sometimes. We can reduce our Christian lives to legalism, and about the most silly as well as serious things. 'If we don't sing that hymn to that tune, I'm not singing it.' 'Communion is done this way, any other way isn't right.' 'If I say that prayer exactly right, it will be more powerful, and God will hear it.' Professing to be good disciples, we can also become antinomians. 'I will persist in this sin, but I will keep praying for forgiveness straight afterwards.' 'What I do with my money, or my body, or my time doesn't count. As long as I say my prayers and turn up in church…'

Both of which have the same effect on us today as on the Philippians Paul wrote to. We live our lives in a way that rejects or opposes the lordship of Jesus Christ over the whole of our lives – body, mind, spirit. He is not Lord of it all.

The remedy is not, however, to be part legalist and part antinomian – the usual compromise. Rather it is, says Paul, to live as citizens of heaven. Those who, if we live as we should as disciples of Jesus, fulfil our responsibilities as citizens of heaven

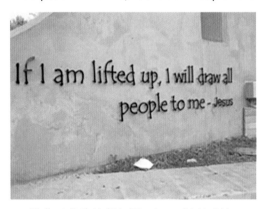

*Wall art. Seth Mokitimi Seminary, SA. M. Atkins*

and earth. In the here and now, this week, in our lives, we live as those for whom Jesus is Lord – Lord of heaven and earth. Of it all. Of all of us. Every part of our lives. Is Jesus Lord of all – of you?

In North West England there used to be Tommy Ball's shoe shops. A 'stack them high, sell them cheap' kind of shoe shop. They used to hang the shoes up on the wall on pegs. They did it by using an airgun to shoot a string through the heels. So you could always tell when someone had bought shoes from Tommy Ball's because of the little holes in the heels. One day a man walked into a shoe shop and plonked a pair of shoes on the customer services desk. 'I've brought these back,' he said, 'I can't walk right in them.' 'I'm sorry about that sir,' said the member of staff, 'What seems to be the problem? Don't they fit?' 'Oh, they fit fine,' replies the man. 'It's the string, it's not long enough!'

So do we keep hobbling or do we cut the string? Some of us need to cut the strings to both legalism and antinomianism, to all lifestyles which are enemies of the cross. But some of us know we can't cut the string for ourselves. We need someone to do it for us, to help us walk right. So as we walk through this holy season of Lent, as we approach the Lord's table and eat bread and wine, examine yourselves, amend what you can of your life, and ask the Lord Christ to release and rectify what you cannot do yourself. So that we become, slowly but surely, a people for whom Jesus Christ is Lord of All. Amen.

# 29

# GARDENS

A sermon for Passiontide.

Reading: Mark 14:32-38.

Well, we're deep into Lent. It's the season that helpfully prevents us moving from Ash Wednesday to Easter Day too quickly and too easily. In these latter days of Lent we focus increasingly on the events immediately leading up to Jesus' entry into Jerusalem and his death and resurrection.

Two favourite places Helen and I like to visit are Kew Gardens and Chelsea Physic Garden. Gardens are wonderful places. According to Genesis, God created the world like a garden. Eden. Paradise. And when you walk round a beautiful garden, it can take your breath away.

But Mollie wouldn't go into her garden. The district nurse encouraged her to sit in it, in the summer months, surrounded by colour and scent. 'It'll do you the world of good,' she said. But Mollie wouldn't. She'd never been back in their garden since the day she'd brought a cup of tea out to Reg, and found him dead among the flowers he was tending.

Gardens can be beautiful places, and painful places.

So by the time we get to the garden of Gethsemane in the story of Jesus we're needing to remind ourselves to revise the 'garden of Eden' imagery, to realise that to be in some gardens isn't to be in paradise, but to be in a place of suffering and searching. You see that in some people's eyes, as they walk through Kew, with that preoccupied, far-away look. Gardens are powerful places. Evocative places. They open the floodgates of our memory. No wonder so many crematoria have gardens of remembrance around them.

And a servant in the house of the high priest, where Jesus has been taken after his arrest, spots a man, over there, hovering, agitated, angry. He walks across to him and says, *'Didn't I see you with him in the garden?'* And Peter's mind explodes with recent memories.

Have we ever been to the garden? Thousands of Christ's followers would have to say, 'No.' Lots of people witnessed Jesus' wonderful deeds – as many of us have. Lots of people heard his gracious words – as many of us have. Lots of people revelled in the parable stories – as many of us have. Lots of people cried 'Hosanna' – as many of us have. But most have never reached the garden in the Christian story. Out of the thousands who met Jesus a small proportion follow him. Sometimes they amount to a crowd, buoyant, optimistic. But by the time Jesus turns his face to Jerusalem many have turned away. By the time he gets to Gethsemane, eleven are with him. Eight hesitate, so only three enter the garden with him. And they fall asleep.

It's like watching a danceathon, as people slowly tire and leave the dance floor, exhausted. Spectators soon outnumber participants. Or like watching a game of poker. As the stakes get ever higher, more and more players fold their hands and come out of the game.

Some folk gather round the manger and look at the infant Jesus, and that is where they – and their Christian faith – remain. Infants round an infant. Some folk make careful study of the teachings of Jesus – but the living of their lives gives little indication that they've ever actually heard or received his teaching. Some folk are caught up with the idealism of the gospel and remain forever idealists – but not disciples. And some folk begin to live the Christian life, they worship in the assemblies, share fellowship in the houses, from time to time set their faces to Jerusalem. But few enter Gethsemane. Few disciples are with him there.

And yet. And yet for every Christian there's the invitation – or is it necessity? – to 'go into the garden.' Although it's a place where few venture, it's a crucial place for all followers of Jesus, because it's in the garden that themes at the heart of gospel, themes so often neglected today, take centre stage. Three things, briefly.

First. It's a place of *selflessness*. Today there's so much emphasis upon our feelings, whether *we* feel the benefit of being a Christian, whether it will help *us*. Too often our worship becomes almost entertainment, evaluated primarily by how we feel about it. Too often our Christian living becomes a mishmash of devotion, custom, and habits not profoundly shaped by the gospel. Too often our Christian service is carefully calculated to consist of what we actually like to do, rather than what we don't, but know is right. It's all about us. Our feelings, our time, our commitment, our likes and dislikes.

It's in Gethsemane that such selfishness is reversed. In Jesus, we see complete selflessness. We're reminded of just how things really are. Of who is who and what is what. The garden shines a spotlight into the soul and illuminates self-serving play-acting. That's why so few venture there. Though it is a necessary place to be from time to time.

Second, it's a place of *surrender*. Have you ever played that after-dinner game when you have to justify why you should be allowed to survive at the expense of others – have the one remaining parachute or whatever? It's in the garden that the One who had more claim to live than any other submits and surrenders to the will of God. It's in Gethsemane that Jesus fights and wins the inner battle about ultimate control in his life. 'Not my will be done, but yours' are the hardest seven words anyone can ever say about their life. Being in the garden is about loosing (not necessarily losing)

179

control of your life, cutting the Gordian knot of self-serving, and handing it, handing yourself, to God. To surrender what you could be to God, if you used your God-given talents in another way, is a hallmark of Gethsemane.

Third, it's a place of *suffering*. We don't know what to make of suffering nowadays, do we? Our advertising suggests life should be permanently a cruise, or flawless skin, or size six figures. Our obsession with perfection means that at one level all illness, weakness or abnormality is viewed as something to be eradicated, put right, or if not, put away. (And yes, I am as supportive as anyone about seeking cures for cancers, etc.)

But in Lent we see the power and necessity of redemptive suffering – the inevitable suffering that comes by seeking to heal, to love, to lay down your life. The suffering that comes about not because you actively seek it, but which arrives because of your commitment to the truth, or because you involve yourself with the lives of others who are suffering.

The life of Jesus bears witness to the key place of redemptive healing – suffering. Without such suffering there's no gospel: we sometimes act as if there is any suffering, then there can't be gospel. Gethsemane sees the Son of God in torment. That is the *skandalon* of the Christian faith, and to many it is still a stumbling block to actually understanding what Christianity is about. Too often we want life without the pain of childbirth. We want eternal life without having to die. We want to ride into Jerusalem and be raised to life without the trauma of Holy Week. We want resurrection faith with a bloodless cross and no garden of suffering.

Have we been to the garden? Or is ours a faith without tears? If so, the New Testament knows little of our kind of Christianity. It takes faith and courage to enter there. But enter it we must. It's in the garden that we're reminded again that being a follower of Jesus is not a hobby. For it's in the garden that disciples find issues are clarified, souls are forged, decisions are made, struggles come to resolution, the will of God is made known more fully, strength is given, and Jesus is known more completely than we might think possible.

But – and it's a big but, so please hear it – we're not in the same situation as Jesus. In the garden, his disciples left him. But he never leaves his disciples. So actually the question isn't 'Have you been to the garden?' but 'Have you been to the garden *with him*?' Because his presence makes all the difference in the world. Jesus

*Live berries, dead grass. Campagna, Italy. H. Atkins*

says to us, 'It's a hard thing, life. But come with me and we'll go through it together. You cannot know what will happen, but you can know that I am with you. Always.'

This Lenten season the call comes again, though few relish it. Jesus asks, 'Will you come into the garden with me?' Or, put another way, Jesus is saying to us, 'Are you going to be my shape, or do you think I'm going to be yours? Which way round shall it be?' His way of being obedient to God is the way of Gethsemane, and the cross, and finally resurrection. Our way so often just isn't! But to all who desire to walk with him, he will show the way and give the strength. Onward to Jerusalem, and the garden, and the grave, and finally – when the time is right – the glory! Amen.

# 30

# AN EXTRAORDINARY DAY (GOOD FRIDAY)

The only sermon in this collection not preached in Methodist Central Hall, Westminster but in Westminster Abbey. For many years, members of MCHW, Westminster Abbey and Westminster Cathedral have joined together in a walk of witness on Good Friday. The silent procession, following a large cross carried by members of The Passage – London's largest voluntary sector resource centre for homeless and vulnerable men and women – stops at all three places of worship where a short address is given and prayers offered.

*Dead leaf cross. H. Atkins*

*'But we preach Christ crucified: a stumbling block to Jews and foolishness to Gentiles, but to those whom God has called, both Jews and Greeks, Christ the power of God and the wisdom of God.'* (1 Corinthians 1:23-24)

Good Friday is by any account an extraordinary day. Like all brutal, profound, complex, tragic, unjust, and mysterious events, it isn't apprehended or understood easily

183

or quickly. The Christian Church has, right down to today, sought to understand and proclaim 'Christ crucified,' but on the first Good Friday, as Jesus' mother, his disciples and the wider group of women and men followers watch on; as the gory, degrading, inhuman events related in all the gospels unfold, and Jesus is slowly and cruelly executed, there would only be shock, horror, heartache, grief and loss. And perhaps among some, bitter disappointment that the one they hailed as a king – the one they believed to be the rescuer from the Roman rule – has failed so spectacularly in that mission.

Had the first Good Friday been happening today, TV crews from around the world would no doubt record the emotions of those caught up in the events of the cross, in much the same way as those caught up in the recent tragic terror attacks in Europe. The crucifixion is a violent, deadly event, and initial responses to it are visceral. The theologising and ruminating about what Jesus' death might mean would come in due course, but later than Good Friday. On the first Good Friday, not Peter, James and John, not Mary – Jesus' mother, Mary Magdalene or any of the other women who figure so prominently in the Easter story would look into the camera and say, 'We are witnessing the greatest act of sacrificial love the world has ever seen. God in Christ is the expiation of the sins of the whole world, and in this death is the hope of humanity, once, for all.' Today the camera just captures them distraught, bereaved and broken. They've walked the real-life version of the events marked by the fourteen Stations of the Cross, and they're beside themselves.

And today, though many of us have lived through the story many times, to its glorious, wonderful outcome on Easter Day, it's fitting for us to allow the raw brutality exerted over an innocent man, who we have come to love and believe to be the Son of God, reach our hearts and minds again, and be moved in our spirits by the sheer humanity, the majesty of self-giving sacrifice of Jesus Christ, and what happened to him on this day so long ago.

But meditating about what Jesus' death on the cross meant to those who believed him to be the Christ began almost immediately and became a central bulwark of Christian faith. And if it was imagined that these meditations and reflections would make their understanding of his death more palatable, or rational to the people of the time, that isn't what happened. St. Paul, writing in the early New Testament book we call 1 Corinthians, wrote this: *'But we proclaim Christ crucified, a stumbling-block to Jews and foolishness to Gentiles, but to those who are the called, both Jews and Greeks, Christ the power of God and the wisdom of God. For God's foolishness is wiser than human wisdom.'* The word translated as 'stumbling block' comes from the Greek *scandalon,* which, apart from helping us get the word 'scandal,' means more literally the thing we trip over, that idea or principle we just cannot 'get,' the faith proposition over which we fall, which stubs not so much our toe as our mind and spirit.

Jewish religious thought – generically rather than specifically – resists the idea that Jesus is the Christ, Messiah, and a key reason for the resistance is that he was crucified, and crucifixion is a defiled, sinners' death. 'So how can that be?' 'Well, it can't be!' 'So this Jesus cannot be the Christ,' goes the logic. Christ crucified, a stumbling block to Jewish thought and faith… and *foolishness* to the Gentiles. Meaning that it's insanity to the many faith groupings spread abroad the Greco-Roman world at the time of Jesus. 'Foolishness,' meaning that which makes no sense at all. An affront to thinking, wise people. An insult to our intelligence. 'How can God's Son suffer?' 'How can the divine experience human trials? 'How can God die?' 'This is just nonsense,' goes the logic.

Faced with this acute resistance, coming in stereo, or more accurately, surround sound, the early followers of Jesus don't do what many would, given the circumstances. They don't rewind, recant, water down, temper their preaching, or build easy bridges. They're gracious but non-apologetic. They declare to both Jews and Greeks – in other words, *everyone* – who 'sees,' who makes the leap of faith and believes, that what happens on Good Friday is God's supreme act of powerful, sacrificial, self-giving, saving grace for the whole planet.

To those who, right down to today, for whom Jesus' life and death is thought a stumbling block, the faithful of Christ say gently, 'We've not found him as One who makes us stumble, but the One who enables us to stand and kneel, and walk and live.' And to those of us right down to today for whom Jesus' life and death seems intellectual foolishness, the wise ones of Christ say to us, 'We've not found believing in him to be nonsense, but in entrusting ourselves to him have found him to be the One who has opened our minds, captured and made safe our souls, deepened our humanity, and transformed our lives.'

'So if we are fools,' say millions of Christian people down the centuries, 'then we are contentedly and gratefully "fools for Christ's sake."' So on this extraordinary day, be wise. Come to the cross, for Christ, its broken, victorious One will receive you. Come be a fool as well! Amen.

# 31

# CHOOSE LIFE!

A good deal of this sermon is borrowed with permission from Bishop Elaine Stanovsky, of the Greater Northwest Area of the United Methodist Church. She herself delivered it at the General Conference in 2016. I incorporated its stimulating imagery into a sermon on Easter Sunday.

Readings: Matthew 27:62 to 28:10, Joshua 4:19-24 & 5:9.

In my youth fellowship we used to sing a song. It went like this:

> The angel rolled the stone away!
> The angel rolled the stone away!
> It was early Easter Sunday morning.
> The angel rolled the stone away!

Well that's Matthew's account of this momentous resurrection day, and it's the account we're focusing on today. It's only Matthew who tells us that the tomb is guarded and sealed, that there's an earthquake, and that an angel comes from heaven and rolls the stone away. Alleluia! Christ is risen! (He is risen indeed! Alleluia!)

Matthew also tells how two women come to the tomb early in the morning and there are three big surprises. One, the tomb isn't sealed with a big round stone. It's open. Two, the women discover not Jesus but an angel. Three, when they do find Jesus, he's not dead. He's alive. And from that moment on begins a small group of people, now a great world faith, who believe that Jesus Christ, the loved and obedient Son of God, could not be killed off but passed over from death to life.

*Passed over* from death to life... The idea of *passing over* and crossing over from death to life lies deep in the biblical story of course. Remember the Old Testament story of how God's people are delivered from slavery in Egypt – the Exodus? Pharaoh won't let the Israelites go, so ten plagues fall upon Egypt, and the last plague is the death of the firstborn in every home in the land. But God 'passes over' – spares – the families of God's people. So, to this day, Jews remember the Passover each year. It's this celebration of deliverance from slavery and captivity, this celebration of rescue from death and the promise of life that Jesus and his disciples are celebrating in what we call the Last Supper – the meal just before his own death and resurrection.

Then the people get to the Red Sea, with Pharaoh's army bearing down on them, and they cross over it – from death to life. Pharaoh's troops shake with fear and become as dead men, as they're overtaken by an act of God and the divided waters of the Red Sea crash down on them... just as troops guarding Jesus' tomb shake with fear and become as dead men as another act of God quakes the earth, and an angel of the Lord crashes down the stone.

Then, after forty long years of wilderness wanderings, the people of God cross over again, over the Jordan River and into the Promised Land. From death to life.

So when Jesus crosses over from death to life that first Easter, these early disciples slowly begin to understand. It's like being delivered from death, released from slavery, entering into the promise of life. Do you see?

There are other echoes going on between this gospel text and the Old Testament too. Matthew tells us that Jesus was crucified at Golgotha, which, he says, means 'the place of a skull.' Golgotha comes from the Hebrew *gulgoleth*, meaning a round skull shape.

# CHOOSE LIFE!

So when the angel rolls away a round skull-like stone to reveal an empty tomb, there is for the Jewish converts to Christ for whom Matthew wrote his gospel, a faint echo of *Gilgal*.

Where? Gilgal. Remember our reading from Joshua? Gilgal. The place the Israelites camped after they first crossed over the Jordan River. The place where they built a memorial of round skull-shaped stones. A memorial declaring that they had crossed over from the death of Egypt into the land of promise and life, a place given them by God. And it is at Gilgal, with its twelve round skull-shaped stones, that God says to Joshua, '*Today I have rolled away the reproach of Egypt from you.*' And the Hebrew word we translate as 'rolled away' is *galal* – meaning 'wheel' – that which is rolled away – like a stone.

Now do we hear the echoes? Galal. Gilgal. Gulgoleth. Golgotha. Stone. Round. Skull. Rolled. Away. Rescue. Spared. Promise. Death. Life. We don't hear it very well, because we don't know the original languages or the biblical stories well enough. But the people Matthew wrote for, steeped in Jewish tradition, they heard it. They got it. Matthew is declaring that the resurrection of Jesus is a new story of God bringing life from death, rooted in ancient stories of God bringing life from death.

But Matthew is an evangelist – that's what we call the writers of the gospels. So he's telling the story of the resurrection of Jesus and  expecting a response from us. He's saying, 'Do you believe Jesus is dead, or that Christ is risen?' He's laying a choice before us: 'Death or life?' And he's urging *us*, we who have heard his words this Easter Day, to choose to believe in and follow the risen Christ – to choose life.

Now when the gospel writers tell us the story of the death and resurrection of Jesus, they present us with 'goodies' and 'baddies'. Unsurprisingly, the baddies are against Jesus and the goodies are for Jesus. Baddies reject who Jesus is and goodies accept who Jesus is. Baddies choose death and goodies choose life.

So when Matthew tells us about the first Easter, he contrasts

189

between the goodies and the baddies, between the women and the guards. Both gather at Jesus' tomb. Both see an angel. Both feel fear. Both leave the tomb to tell others what's happened. Both are told what they should say. The stark difference is that the women tell the truth to the disciples, and the guards tell a lie *about* the disciples. Two completely different responses to the resurrection of Jesus. Goodies and baddies.

Matthew tells us quite a lot about the baddies. Imagine, it's the morning after the crucifixion, and the Jewish leaders file into Pilate's court. 'Sir, Jesus isn't dead enough yet!' they say. 'What do you mean?' says Pilate. 'He said he would rise again,' they say. 'So wouldn't it be a good idea to seal that tomb, to prevent anyone from sneaking in and stealing his body and saying he's alive. That'd cause a lot of trouble. We both need him dead and staying dead.' So soldiers march to the tomb, seal it, and stand guard, like sentries at Buckingham Palace.

Then there's the goodies. It's morning and evening, the third day. It's sunrise, and two women come to the tomb, desperately sad, longing that somehow his death on the cross hasn't ended the promise of Jesus. And an angel of God falls out of heaven. There's an earthquake and lightning. The guards quake and fall. The angel rolls away the mighty round stone and sits on it. 'I will decide,' says the angel of the Lord God, 'who comes and goes from this tomb: who lives and who dies.' The women look in and the tomb is empty. And they run away, afraid, bewildered – but with the beginnings of great joy.

So Matthew presents us with two versions of what happened. The chief priests and Pharisees say Jesus is dead. 'We killed him. We sealed the tomb. We set the guard. It's sorted,' they say. But the women say – and quickly, though not instantly, all the disciples join them in saying – 'He's not dead. Jesus is risen!' Alleluia!

Evangelist Matthew repeats his challenge and choice to readers down the ages, and this Easter morning to us. Are you like those who deny life, and repress truth – even when it escapes the tomb right in front of you? Or are you like the women, and the other disciples, who follow Jesus on the 'life' side of the tomb?

As Christ's Church we sometimes choose death over life. We sometimes choose to live in the tomb rather than following into the world where the risen Jesus lives. Sometimes we live our lives as if we were still in the tomb. We call it sin: thinking and acting and living as if Jesus was still dead and buried. And the angel of God says to us, 'Why do you seek the living among the dead?' Jesus lives. He's left the tomb. 'He is not here,' says the angel. And if you want to be with Jesus you must leave the tomb behind too. You must choose life.

This Easter Day I say to us all that we don't have to stay in slavery to sins or addictions. Cross over – choose life! We don't have to wander in the wilderness forever. Cross over – choose life! We needn't stay entombed with fear and death. Cross over – choose life! We can choose to believe that Jesus Christ is risen – choose life! We can choose to live with him, here and now, as companion and Lord. We can choose life!

*Easter cross outside MCHW. H. Atkins*

Oh, we'll all die. Someday. Be sure about that. But this Easter be equally sure it won't be the end of everything. The same life-giving God who delivered his people from slavery to freedom, from despair to hope, from death to life, is the same God who raised Jesus the Son to life. The same God who says to you and to me, 'Choose life! Choose my Christ. Choose to follow him before your death, and by my power follow him at the day of your resurrection. And then forever and ever.' Alleluia! Amen.

# 32

# COMMISSIONED BY JESUS?

I love the Easter season, taking us through Ascension Day to Pentecost. Over the years I've found myself returning again and again to the resurrection appearances of the risen Christ. Consequently, several sermons of this type and topic are included here, and I've preached them as a mini-series. In this sermon some of the allusions to life at Richmond College almost certainly originate from my good friend Revd. Dr. Howard Mellor, former Principal of Cliff College.

Readings: Matthew 28:16-20 & Colossians 1:3-8.

Today we look at one of the most famous – and probably most preached – passages in the New Testament. It's from the very end of Matthew's gospel and is widely known as the Great Commission, but probably not until the 17th century was it known in that way. Protestant Reformers and many earlier Christian leaders and thinkers understood this commission of Jesus to be given only to the disciples with Jesus at the time. So when the last apostle died, the apostolic commission died with it. A Great Commission for the special, but very few.

John Wesley died in March 1791, and only a year later, in 1792, a young cobbler, a Baptist, went to a group that was to evolve to become the Baptist Missionary Society. The cobbler had written a booklet with a not-too-pithy title: *An Enquiry into the Obligations of Christians to use Means for the Conversion of the Heathens.* It argued that the command of Jesus to make disciples given in Matthew 28 is binding on all Christians and not just the original disciples on the mountain. One person at the meeting, John Ryland, is famously reported to have said to William Carey – for that is who the young cobbler was – 'Sit down young man, when God pleases to convert the heathen, he will do it without aid from you or me.' A typically Calvinist response of the period. But Carey won the day and the age of Protestant missions effectively began to move through the gears.

John Wesley wasn't the first, but he was an early adopter to preach on this passage as if it was a command of Jesus to us, now, as well as to them, then. And I romantically wonder whether theologically Arminian Christians like Wesley influenced theologically Calvinist Christians in slowly coming to accept that actively seeking to make disciples of Christ was the duty and privilege of all Christians. 'God saves whom he wills,' said some Christians. 'Yes,' said others, 'but God wills all to be saved.' And it was in this broad and complex context that the passage from the end of Matthew began to be called the Great Commission.

I want us to look at this passage today and note a few things.

First, notice that Jesus tells his followers to 'Go!' So what, you say? Simply that I note how much of our life today as Christians is configured around inviting people to come to us. But from Easter Day, and increasingly from Pentecost, Christianity is demonstrably an 'outward-facing' religion – a 'Go!' faith.

We've often associated *going* with mission *overseas*, rather than on our doorstep. When in fact culturally, socially and religiously, there's such a need for us today to go into our local neighbourhoods and communities. That is why I'm so much a supporter of Fresh Expressions of Church – as Christ's we are a people on the move rather than a set and sedentary church congregation waiting for folk to beat a path to our doors. How wonderful it will be when each and every local church is committed to planting new churches and congregations! How fantastic it will be when rather than just closing churches, we close them in order to begin something else, something new, something nearer to the large majority of people who don't yet know Jesus as loving Lord and strong Saviour, and have no demonstrable interest in his Church!

I often wish we had the demonstrable faith and commitment of the early Methodist missionaries. Many of them trained at Richmond College in West London. Today, if you visit Methodist Church House on Marylebone Road, there's a Richmond Room, named after the college. Because several large wooden boards listing many of the earlier Wesleyan Methodist missionaries found their way there after the college closed in 1971. The boards cover a region of the world to which the missionaries went. They list the names, the year they went to serve and the year they died.

No wonder West Africa was called the white man's grave! On that board is name after name where the year the missionary went and the year they died are just a small handful of years apart. 'J.W. Bell – Entered College 1872. Died 1874.' I'm told the

*Africa board, Methodist Church House. M. Atkins*

trainee missionaries began to make their own wooden chests in which to put all their belonging on the boat, and made them of a size to be a coffin because they knew they wouldn't be coming back. I'm told that at their weekly communion service when the Principal read out the names of those who'd died, and paused and prayed, and then asked those who would go in their stead to stay behind for a commissioning prayer

195

at the communion rail, there were always those who stayed, symbolically saying, 'I'll go.' And they went.

Now we don't all need to become missionaries overseas – times have changed and not all for the worse – but we do need to remind ourselves that Jesus said 'Go,' not 'Settle down,' and that command still stands and is given to us, here, now.

Go… *and make disciples.*

Jesus didn't say 'You go build my Church and I will make disciples.' He said, 'I will build my Church and you go make disciples.' How much we need to keep remembering that! And note too that Jesus said to make disciples, not converts. Disciples. Those for whom following Jesus Christ is life-long and about every aspect of life. Those for whom Christianity is not simply life-enhancing but life transforming. Those who become free samples of the gospel, rather than, as we often are portrayed, salespeople of corporate Christianity. Making Christian disciples is a key work of the Church.

Go and make disciples *of all nations…*

There are times when translating New Testament Greek to English does us no favours at all, and this is one of them. 'Nations,' in terms of nation states, arose, particularly in Europe, about the same time people were deciding that this passage in Matthew could be referred to as the Great Commission. So when we hear 'nations' that's what most of us think of – that's why we so easily relate the call to mission to go other countries in the world. But *panta ta ethne* – to use the original Greek words – doesn't mean 'nations' in the sense of Germany or China, but rather all people, of all races, in all places, of all ages, and all stages. In short, everyone. Every generation of Christians has trouble with this passage, because it gives us no help whatsoever in our endless search to find people to exclude!

*Baptising and teaching them to obey everything I have commanded you.*

I want to focus briefly on the 'teaching' bit. Because again I don't think the common understanding of the word does us many favours. Methodism is a branch of Christianity born in the cultural era known as the Enlightenment, when to learn something was to be taught it in a particular way. When I first became a Christian I was given a booklet – *Journey into Life*, by Norman Warren. By text and simple line drawings it logically laid out for me what I was – a sinner for what I'd done, sinned and disappointed God, and what I now had to do: to give myself to Jesus Christ, declaring him my personal Saviour and Lord. It explained and interpreted it all for me and asked me to agree. And I did. I look back now and don't regret the decision I made for a second. But in light of decades seeking to be a disciple of Jesus it all now seems a bit 'tick boxy.' Becoming a Christian was closely associated with mental assent to this and that doctrine. 'Do you believe this?' 'Yes.' 'Tick!'

I probably overstate the case to make it, but I don't think that kind of teaching is what's being referred to here, when Jesus says 'teaching them.' Jesus is a rabbi, a teacher. And the rabbi taught not just propositions for acceptance or rejection, but through a parable, word, deed, lifestyle. So 'teaching all I have commanded you' certainly includes teaching, and learning certain things and holding to them, but equally certainly it is a command to go and be like Jesus. So that as people encounter us, Christ's people, individually and together, they feel they're drawing near to Jesus himself. What a calling!

*And I am with you always...*

Do you remember the name given to Jesus at his birth, found only in Matthew's gospel? He is to be called 'Emmanuel' which means 'God is with us.' And here, at the end of that gospel Jesus, Emmanuel, says, '*I am with you...*'

I want to suggest a little heresy! I've often wondered whether or not '*I am with you always*' is a conditional promise. Because the New Testament Greek permits as easily a conditional statement – *If you go*, *if* you make disciples of all peoples, and *if* you teach all that I have commanded by being like me, *then* I will be with you always, with the implication that if we don't heed and obey his instructions, we can't rely on the promise. In which case the best thing to do is to ensure we do fulfil his Great Commission!

Let's return to the boards listing the names of Methodist missionaries in Methodist Church House. When I worked in that building I'd show them to visiting ministers from around the world. 'When did they die?' asked one person I showed round. I thought it was obvious, but wanted to be polite. 'Well you see the name, and look in the last column. John Doe, went to Sierra Leone in 1826, died 1828. He died in 1828.' Or did he? Or did he die when he stayed behind after communion at Richmond College, and said, 'I'll go'? Or did he die when he first felt the call to be Christ's missionary? Or did he die when he first responded to Christ many years earlier? You see, the Great Commission is given by the Living One Who Died, and has been taken up down the centuries by other living ones who have 'died.' And Christ requires in each generation, in each place – in this church, at this time, us, you, me – to choose to die to self and live for Christ, and receive the Great Commission as given to us. Pray we have the courage to receive it and live it out. Amen.

# 33

# PEACE BE WITH YOU

Readings: John 20:19-29 & John 6:16-21.

Many years ago my eldest son came into the lounge looking a bit sheepish. 'Dad, can you come look at the car?' he said. It was pranged and finished up being written off. I looked at the car, he looked at the car, I looked at him, he looked at me then said, 'I know what you're going to say!' Then one day my elderly mother rang me. She was very upset. She'd fallen and was on the floor. So, I hurried over to her house and helped her up. She was a bit shaken but after a cup of tea was fundamentally fine. 'What were you doing?' I asked. 'I was trying to move the bed to clean behind it,' she said. I looked at her, and she looked at me and said, 'I know what you're going to say!'

Then there are some disciples. In a locked room. Desolate. They've denied and deserted their friend. They've let their Lord down. They watched, helpless and horrified as he was put to death. They feel they'll carry their guilt all their lives. And the risen Jesus comes into their locked room. They look at him, and he looks at them, and they wince inside and think, 'We know what he's going to say!' And what does he say? 'Peace be with you.' I suspect that the only sound in the room was a loud 'Phew' by a group of men breathing a huge sigh of relief. I wonder if that's what they expected him to say. I wonder if, much later when they're talking together they said, 'We never expected that.'

199

But so often Jesus says things more gracious, more surprising, and more forgiving than we expect or deserve. When we rightly cringe and fear the worst, that's not what happens. The prodigal son returns home with his tail between his legs and a prepared speech. He doesn't get to the end of the first sentence before his father hugs him. And later, after the party, I wonder if the son reflected on the day and said, 'I never expected that.' Or the woman caught in adultery, knowing the law and expecting the worst. 'I don't condemn you,' says Jesus, 'now go and sin no more.' And she does, pinching herself that she's alive, shaking her head and saying to herself, 'I never expected that!'

And before we all get on our self-righteous hobby horses, how would we like to be treated by Jesus Christ? As we deserve, or with mercy and grace? I don't know about you, but I'll take mercy and grace every time!

Do you know the most frequent sentiment in the Bible? Be good? Be holy? Attend the leadership team meeting? No. It's this. 'Fear not.' 'Don't be afraid.' 'It is I.' 'Peace be with you.' The root, the related meaning of all these phrases is the same. So really, 'Peace be with you' is just typical. Amazing. But amazingly typical.

John's gospel has a special way of understanding peace. All four gospels contain a version of the occasion when Jesus and the disciples cross a lake, and there's a storm. The best known versions are in the synoptic gospels. Jesus is asleep – on a cushion Mark says – the storm erupts, the disciples are frightened and Jesus is woken up. Jesus stills the storm and then tells them off, or the other way round, depending on the gospel. In one account Jesus says, 'Peace, be still.'

John's version of the stilling of the storm is different. The disciples are in the boat on their own when the storm comes. Jesus comes across the water through the storm and says to them, 'It is me. Don't be afraid.' And, we're told, immediately, they reach the peace and security of the shore.

# PEACE BE WITH YOU

In the synoptic gospels Jesus stills the storm, and there is peace. In John's gospel, Jesus comes in the midst of the storm, and there is peace.

Some years ago a regional art competition took place and all entrants had to submit pictures on the theme of peace. The second prize was given to a lovely watercolour which captured the tranquility of the Lake District, with its mirror image between water and sky. You looked at it and went, 'Aaahh.' The picture that won first prize had people scratching their heads. It was a large oil painting, with roiling dark clouds and rolling dark waves. And dominating the painting, off to one side was a large, needle-like rock, wet and battered by stormy waves. Most people had to look at it for a while before seeing that there, in the midst of the storm, on the sheltered side of the rock, in a small cranny, was one seabird, fast asleep. And like all the pictures, this was called 'Peace.' We might say that the synoptic gospels got second prize and John's gospel got first!

Some of us have had experiences where the storm has been stilled, the source of unrest or anxiety or pain taken away, and we received peace. For some of us the source of pain and suffering remained, but Jesus came to us, and there was in some wonderful, real way, peace in the storm. Both are God's gift.

You see, whether it's Jesus walking through the storm to frightened disciples, or the risen Jesus walking into a locked room to frightened disciples, Jesus brings peace. His presence brings peace. He is peace. Because peace isn't abstract, it's intensely personal. A parent doesn't say to a frightened child, 'I'm going downstairs and I'll bring you back some peace.' Your child will say, 'Don't go away mummy (or daddy)!' You embody peace. And it's the same with the Lord. To frightened disciples, in various storms, behind all sorts of closed doors, he comes. And he embodies the words he says. 'It's alright. I'm here. Peace be with you.'

'"Peace be with you"… and he showed them his hands and his side.' Even on the risen Jesus is the evidence of his death. This is not a sci-fi movie where a blown to bits resuscitated corpse reappears as if their grisly death never was. The risen Jesus isn't physically perfect, He's the living one... who died. You can see the marks of his death.

There's a cost to peace. Grace, forgiveness, the offer of peace, isn't cheap or painless. Talk to peacekeepers in Israel, Palestine, Syria or Ireland about the price of peace. Talk to some of those to whom life-changing things have happened, because of the violence or abuse of others, and how – incredibly – they talk about forgiveness and what's involved in pursuing peace amidst a seemingly never-ending storm. It costs. It involves sacrifice, self-giving. And it cost Christ. And you see in him the costly signs of offering peace.

It's to those who begin to see the cost of peace that Jesus gives a command. 'As the Father has sent me, so I send you.' This was the late great Lesslie Newbigin's favourite 'great commission' of Jesus. He used to say that every word of the sentence was important, but that the most important word was 'as'. It means 'like.' 'Like the Father has sent me... so I am sending you.' In other words, the commission to dying and rising, to self-giving and sacrifice, to preaching and teaching and healing, to making and offering his peace is given to these frightened, bewildered disciples. Just as that ministry is given to his disciples today. To us.

So, today we're invited to hear two things. First, Jesus saying to us 'peace be with you' – so that whether the storm ceases or it continues, we know the peace Jesus brings to us and is for us. But also that we not only receive peace, but be ourselves people of peace. 'Like him' people. People filled with his presence. People who in his name say to others in word and deed, 'Peace be with you.' Amen.

# 34

# BREAKFAST WITH JESUS

Yet another Easter season sermon! On this occasion, the text is used chiefly to pose a series of questions which together seek to diagnose the liveliness of our faith and elicit our positive responses.

Reading: John 21:1-14.

Today we look at another of the occasions when the risen Jesus comes to his disciples. We're in John's gospel, chapter 21, which, we're told, is the third time Jesus appears to them. I want us to look at this vivid story of fishing and breakfast with Jesus, and use it to inquire about our Christian health and discipleship. So we pray: Lord, open your holy Word to our lives and our hearts, and our lives and our hearts to your holy Word. Amen.

'*Jesus appeared again to the disciples…*' I love that word again. *Agains* are important. Times when Jesus comes again. How wonderful when we can remember the first time Jesus came to us, when we became aware of his love for us, when we offered our lives to him and the service of God's kingdom. You can call it conversion, being born again, being saved, seeing the light, I don't mind. But equally important are times when Jesus comes to us again. Because faith is a living thing. It begins with a step of faith but it must result in a walk of life.

I confess that I find some testimonies more interesting than others. Testimonies that begin with 'I met the Lord in 1976,' and the story effectively ends in 1976, both bore and worry me. How much more vital is the person who testifies to what happened last week, how the Lord gave peace, or healing, or safety, or blessing, or opportunity, when Jesus came again, and faith became currently real rather than historically remembered? Since I got married about forty years ago, so much has changed. I've changed shape! The clothes I wear, the food I eat, the cars I drive, the places I go on holiday, the appliances in my home have all changed. I expect the same is true for many of you. Every area of our lives has seen huge changes, except, for so many of us in the realm of our faith, where we're living on what we received so long ago. So is it time that you met and experienced the risen Jesus again? If so, I've got good news for you. Jesus is longing to meet you – again.

'*Jesus appeared again… by the sea of Tiberias.*' Or as it's better known, the Sea of Galilee. What on earth are the disciples doing up there? They've gone back! These disciples, several of them once fishermen, but called by Jesus to be fishers of people, have gone back to trying to catch fish. They're like so many of us. We've been called to follow Christ. We profess to be his. We have a gospel to proclaim, we have a mission to fulfil, we have a saviour to live for. But we keep looking over our shoulders. You sometimes heard it in the testimonies I talked about. 'What a big sinner I was,' they say, sometimes almost with relish. Then they almost sigh as they say, 'And then I became a Christian!' They make the sinning sound so much more attractive than the following!

Let me tell you that if you're called by the Lord and you flirt with going back to 'life like it was before,' you're doomed to disappointment. You'll be miserable with the things that once satisfied you. You're not the same, and what you try to return to won't be the same. Jesus effectively says to the disciples, 'Why are you trying to catch fish when I've called you to catch people?' It won't work. Sometimes we're tempted to give up on

204

our discipleship of Jesus. The disciples were at this point, I think. Here we catch a sign of their lost-ness. In this passage in John, I wonder how Peter says, 'I'm going out to fish.' I see him pacing up and down in the midst of a group of bewildered and confused folk. Then suddenly, 'Oh, I'm going fishing!' 'We'll come with you,' they say, relieved, as if they don't know what else to do.

Have you given your life to Christ, and then in subtle ways taken it back? Tried to go back to how it used to be? Perhaps today Jesus is calling you to be obedient to what he has called you to be. Today, can you hear him come to you and say, 'Follow me' – again?

So Peter the ex-fisherman tries to go back to how life was before Jesus. He is, after all, a master fisherman, so he puts the boat out, goes to waters he knows well, puts the nets down and he catches… nothing. All night. Nothing. About dawn, across the water, comes an unknown voice, 'Friends,' (is the word in our translation, but the Greek also hints at 'little ones' or 'children' – immature ones). '*Friends, haven't you caught any fish?*' Now, how do you imagine the disciples say, 'No'? I hear them shout aggressively and fed up – 'No!'

'*Well*,' says the voice, '*put the net down at the other side and you will find some*.' It's amazing that Peter obeys. I mean, what are you like when people tell you how to do something you think you're good at? I'm surprised Peter doesn't shout across the water, 'Listen here. I don't know who you are but I've been fishing these waters all my life. I know where the fish are, now just keep your opinions to yourself and clear off.' That would be more likely. But Peter does as the voice tells him. Which in fishing terms isn't good advice, because there was no rigging on one side to help pull the net back into the boat – which is likely why they had to drag the net ashore to empty it.

Now what's all this about? What's John telling us? That being obedient to Jesus is always fruitful? That our efforts will be fruitless without the Lord? Even if we are experienced or talented at something? You see Peter had to bring the things he knows best under the lordship of Jesus. Most of us are able to offer to God those things we can't do, or can't cope with. It's our gifts and talents we have difficulty giving to God. But we must, if we're to grow as disciples. What was it Charles Wesley wrote? 'My talents, gifts, and graces Lord, into thy blessed hands receive.' Peter, the master fisherman, has to give to the Master what he feels he has mastered, before it really brings forth fruit. What might you have to give back to Christ?

So they put the nets over the wrong side of the boat, and the catch is fantastic. The net is full to bursting. And Peter suddenly realises. The lightbulb moment. The point of revelation. *'It is the Lord,'* he says, and dives into the water and heads for the shore.

I want to pose a simple question: when in your life you realise 'It is the Lord,' which direction do you go? Away from Jesus or towards him? Jonah, for example, runs away from God. The story of Jonah isn't so much about a big fish but more about the internal spiritual problems Jonah has coming to grips with God's call and God's grace. He hears God's call, and he knows 'It is the Lord,' so he boards a ship going in the opposite direction – as far from God as possible.

Now what about Peter? Peter who failed Jesus. Peter who denied Jesus. Was he still wracked with a deep sense of failure and betrayal? I think so. That's one reason why he's here, back by the lakeside. When he hears John say, 'It is the Lord,' bless him, Peter runs towards Jesus. How hard it is to face someone you've wronged! Think for a moment of a person you feel you've disappointed, or conned, or neglected. The person you said you'd ring up – and didn't, write to – and didn't, go visit – and didn't. So when they ring you, or you see them coming down a supermarket aisle, which way do you want to go?

So notice this. The fact that Peter heads towards Jesus tells us still more about Jesus than it does about Peter. It tells us that in spite of all his sense of guilt and failure, Peter knows deep inside that Jesus is someone to whom you can turn again, no matter what the circumstance. Because Jesus is full of grace, compassion, understanding and forgiveness.

Do you need grace, compassion, understanding or forgiveness? A new start? In your life when you become aware, 'It is the Lord,' how does your spiritual body language react? Do you shrink back? Is your sense of failure a barrier? Or like Peter, do you realise the only way forward is to head towards Jesus? You can turn and head towards Jesus this very moment.

One of the characteristics of Jesus' post-resurrection appearances is his desire to feed people.

In this story, eating is a symbol of restored fellowship. It's beside a charcoal fire that Peter denies his Lord, and it's beside a charcoal fire that Jesus offers food for fellowship. To accept it is to accept Jesus' offer of restoration. *'Bring some of the fish you have just caught,'* says Jesus. 'Come and have breakfast.'

From what we know of Peter, he was quite stubborn. 'You won't wash my feet,' he says to Jesus on one occasion. And in the days before the crucifixion: 'Others may leave and desert you, Lord, but I won't.' So you can imagine him here saying something like, 'Feed the others first, Lord. I'm not very hungry… If there's anything left, I'll have it in a while…' 'Peter, eat,' says Jesus. And Peter knows that if he is to have strength for the journey ahead, he must receive all the Lord Jesus gives him. Jesus has never let anyone go hungry who truly hungers after him, and seeks strength to live life in obedience to his will.

Do you let Jesus feed you, or are you on a spiritual hunger strike? *'Behold, I stand at the door and knock,'* said Jesus. Remember? *'If anyone hears my voice and opens the door, I will come in and eat with him and he with me."*

So, brothers and sisters, how long is it since Jesus came 'again'? It can be today. Have you given your life, and then taken it back? Have you gone back to living like it was before, and failed miserably? You can turn again and follow. Have you brought under his lordship what you feel most secure and competent about? Do you hide yourself behind your gifts, when they need to be his gifts? He will transform you again if you ask him. When Christ calls to you, how do you react? Do you turn towards him or away from him? Because, whatever, he will receive you again. Do you let Christ feed you with himself? Or are you still stubborn? He offers himself to you as Saviour and Lord, again, today. Let's do business with God. Amen.

# 35

# SAUL BECOMING PAUL

An Easter season sermon taking up a common theme of lives changed by Jesus Christ, and how they may change.

Readings: Acts 9:1-19 & Philippians 3:4b-11.

I want to talk today about conversion. In particular, a very special, well-known conversion. Arguably no encounter with Jesus Christ has affected the nature of Christianity more than when Saul of Tarsus, a Jew by birth, a Roman by nurture, a Greek by culture, met the risen Jesus on a well travelled highway. Even today, people – Christian and not – talk of life-changing events as a Damascus Road experience.

My sermon today poses three questions to Saul who becomes known as Paul: First, Paul, what kind of person were you? Second, Paul, what happened to you? Third, Paul, what happened to you after that? A sort of before, during and after theme.

'Paul, what kind of person were you?' And I think he may well reply, 'I was a man under conviction.' Why? Because the Christian witness of Stephen the martyr played on his mind. Luke records Stephen's death in Acts 7 and ends with this chilling sentence, '*And Saul approved of their killing him.*' Then in Acts 22:20 we read Paul's testimony. He says, '*And while the blood of your witness Stephen was shed, I myself was standing by, approving and keeping the coats of those who killed him.*' It haunts him. He's under conviction.

Witness matters. Suffering for Christ's sake matters. Bearing witness to faith in Christ in the normal things of life matters. My Sunday School teacher was called Mr Bell. A kindly old man, I and a number of other 8-year-olds made his life a misery, I'm sure. Years after leaving Sunday school, when I became a Christian, I felt the need to find Mr Bell and tell of my decision to become a follower of Jesus, sure he would be thrilled. I discovered that he'd died just months before. Often the one who bears witness to Christ doesn't know its effect. But that doesn't mean it has no effect. You who bear Christian witness to your children and grandchildren, neighbours and workmates may never know its effect, but that doesn't mean it has no effect. Stephen the martyr never knew he had an effect on Saul who became Paul, but he did. So take heart and keep faith with the faith. We may never know the consequences of our witness, but ultimately that's not the most important thing.

But when we ask him what kind of person he was, Paul would probably also say he was a devout, good Jewish man. Remember how he described himself in our reading from Philippians? *'If anyone else has reason to be confident in the flesh, I have more: circumcised on the eighth day, a member of the people of Israel, of the tribe of Benjamin, a Hebrew born of Hebrews; as to the law, a Pharisee; as to zeal, a persecutor of the church; as to righteousness under the law, blameless.'* Modesty was not Paul's greatest gift! But clearly he sees himself as a good Jew. Knowledgeable, moral, zealous, faithful, sincere. A devout man who lived his life pleasing God as he understood it.

I labour this fact because in an attempt to dramatise their conversion experiences some Christians often beef up their sinfulness. 'What a sinner I was, you've no idea what I was like… But now…' But that has an unfortunate effect sometimes, because we inadvertently make it harder to convince knowledgeable, moral, zealous, faithful, sincere people, that they too need Christ. An encounter with Jesus Christ isn't only required by so-called 'big sinners,' but is also required by every knowledgeable, moral, zealous, faithful and sincere person... like most of us. C. S. Lewis wrote, 'What God requires is not just nice people, but new people.'

So to the second question: Paul, what happened to you? And he would reply, 'I met Jesus.' Paul rarely uses *'metanoia(en)'* – the word we translate as 'conversion.' That word is beloved of evangelical preachers – meaning a change of heart and mind and direction. It's a great word, but isn't much used by Paul. Instead, Paul describes his Damascus Road experience as 'the occasion when Jesus appeared to me,' or even better, 'Jesus appeared *in* me.' Meeting Jesus Christ is the quintessential Christian experience for all of us.

I used to be a boy scout. I loved it. I went camping all the time. The camps included competitions for the different scout troops in the area. I remember one test in particular. We were taken to the top of a hill, where there was a large plastic barrel full of water, dozens of empty smaller containers, and a wooden tray fastened by nails to a rope. The rope was about one hundred yards long and meandered down a steep ravine. 'Right,' said the scout leader introducing the test, 'The object is simple. Get as much water as you can on this tray, take it down the ravine, and the troop that gets the most water to the bottom, wins.'

And if I say so myself, we were brilliant! We got the largest containers and filled them from the barrel, using every square inch of the wooden tray. Then we set off down the hill, through bushes, over streams. We got to the bottom and hardly a drop had spilled. We clapped each other on the back, very upbeat. The leader poured the water from all our containers into a big tube to measure it, and we watched it fill up thinking that nobody will beat it.

We got nearly two gallons down the hill. We did beat a couple of other troops, but one troop got seven gallons! Our bubble burst. We even got a bit cross. 'They must have cheated,' we said. 'Did they go up and down three times? How did they do it?' I'll never forget the reply of the slightly smug scout leader. 'Well lads, that large barrel you used to fill all the small containers, they just brought that down here!' You see, what we'd done was excellent within our own rules. But by the rules permitted we came nowhere.

This is Paul's experience. Within the rules of his strict Jewish upbringing and context, he's perfect. Then he meets Jesus and realises he's not perfect. Paul the good Pharisee realises a startling truth. On meeting Jesus Christ, he's got it wrong! In Philippians he continues, *'But whatever gain I had, I counted as loss for the sake of Christ. Indeed, I count everything as loss because of the surpassing worth of knowing Christ Jesus my Lord.'* 'My whole life is based on a mistake,' he says in effect. 'The things I thought were valuable are worthless. The things I thought were significant are like rubbish. The things I thought were worth living for are the wrong things. It's like someone changed all the price tags on everything.'

To talk about a 'moral' conversion as if Paul was 'immoral' is missing the point. To talk about Paul simply changing religious allegiances in a midlife crisis is missing the point. It's more like Paul has a new magnetic north. A new point of reference. And because he has a new magnetic north, every other point on the compass is changed. This brave, devout man finds his life has fundamentally changed direction.

Paul's is more a sudden *surrender* than a sudden conversion. We don't need to be a 'big' sinner to qualify. If you regard yourself as a knowledgeable, moral, zealous, faithful, and sincere person, trying to live a life pleasing to God as you understand it… fine. But to you too I say, meeting Jesus Christ is for you. A Christian is a person who has ceased to do what they want to do and who has begun to do what Jesus Christ wants them to do. Perhaps God is speaking to some of us here today about that.

To the third question: 'Paul, what happened to you after that?' Paul would respond, 'I kept on following Jesus.' Paul kept going. His Damascus Road experience was a beginning, but not an end. Indeed, Paul, the great apostle, who wrote letters and founded churches, and travelled here, there and everywhere, doesn't emerge as a leading figure for well over a decade after he meets Jesus on the road. He disappears off the scene for several years – and I often wonder where he was, and who ministered to him, who enabled Saul to truly become Paul, the apostle to the Gentiles. Whoever they were, they did a great job.

Today, I want you to note just one characteristic of Paul's Christian life. He keeps mixed company. As a Christian his circle of friends and acquaintances widens. By contrast, ours often reduces. His grows: men, women, lowly, important, Jews, Gentiles, Romans, Christians, slaves,

*Have shoes will travel. S. Atkins*

masters. Because Paul came to realise a simple truth – you can't be a witness for Christ if you live in a solely Christian world. Since becoming a Christian, has your friendship network opened up or closed down?

You can tell that Luke, the writer of the Acts, thought that Paul's Damascus Road experience was important, because he relates the story three times – in chapters 9, 22, and 26. And each time the story is told it gets longer! Each time there's more to say. These accounts of Paul's Christian life are like snapshots in a spiritual album. They show a maturing Paul, someone who grows up in faith. It's said that you can count the pips in an apple, but you can't count the apples in a pip!

In his book on St. Paul, Carlo Martini pictures Paul awaiting execution and looking back on his life. He suggests that only when you're at the point of death you know the meaning of your conversion. So in Philippians 3, after laying out what a fine Jewish man he was, and how he came to realise it was all wrong, a mature Christian Paul makes an amazing statement. '*I want to know Christ and the power of his resurrection and the sharing of his sufferings by becoming like him in his death, if somehow I may attain the resurrection from the dead.'* I want to know Christ… Jesus Christ is still the object of his zeal and I wonder if that's true of us.

Having asked some questions of Paul I close by asking some questions to all of us here today. Do you need to meet Jesus? Have you met Jesus? If you have, are you still following Jesus? In a few moments' silence, let's do business with God. Amen.

# SOMEONE UP THERE LOVES YOU (ASCENSION)

**MCHW has a communion service on the evening of Ascension Day itself. This sermon was preached on the Sunday after Ascension.**

**Readings: Luke 24:44-53 & Acts 1:1-11.**

Today we complete what we might call the 'earthly' period of Jesus' life, because we reach the point when Jesus leaves his disciples and ascends into heaven and returns to God the Father. First, we're going to look at what the Ascension of Jesus means, and do a little study and theology together. Don't switch off, it's fun! Then I'm going to tell you some stories that illuminate the nature of the Ascension for us, and I hope they're fun too.

Writers of our soap operas and thriller series all take a lesson from Luke. Each new episode starts with the cliff-hanging end scene from the previous episode. That's what happens here in the two readings. The dramatic scene is the Ascension of Jesus Christ. It's the 'hinge' scene that ends Luke's gospel and then begins the book of Acts. It's Luke – who in both his gospel and the Acts of the Apostles – tells us most about Jesus ascending into heaven. Just as, incidentally, it's Luke's gospel that tells us most about the birth of Jesus and most details about the beginning and the end of the life on earth of Jesus Christ.

The first thing I want you to note is that Luke wants us, his readers, to know that the Ascension of Jesus is important. Without the Ascension Luke implies that Christmas can be understood as a romantic fairytale, that Good Friday can simply be the tragic story of another well-meaning failure, and that Easter can be the mysterious tale about a revived corpse. It's the Ascension that makes clear Jesus' work on earth is done, and his going 'up into heaven,' rather than, say, just disappearing, makes clear that Jesus' crucial work of God is done as *God wanted it done*. The Ascension marks completion and success – not 'done your best, but failed!' It's one of those occasions – and I've spoken about them before – when God draws back the curtains and light floods in, as if God was saying, 'Look. He is who he says he is! I vouch for him. It's okay to believe and obey. I receive him back into heaven with joy. He has done all things well.'

Second, I want you to note that the Ascension of Jesus brings to an end how the disciples of Jesus are able to follow him. Up to now, the following has been quite literally 'being with him,' witnessing his deeds, hearing his words, receiving his teaching, travelling together. From now on their discipleship is going to be different. They'll still be going with him, but in a different way. They'll still be witnessing his deeds, but they are playing a different role. They'll still hear his words, but they will now also declare them. Having received his teaching, they'll now be asked to proclaim it.

Note a pattern in Luke. Jesus spent forty days in the wilderness, communing with God, after which he takes up his ministry in a new way. The disciples spend forty days communing with the risen Jesus who teaches them about the kingdom of God, after which they are to take up his ministry in a new way. Similarly, our discipleship of Jesus and the ministries we exercise in Jesus' name go through different phases. Sometimes, it's our age that determines that, or our health, or some other factors. But the secret of living discipleship is saying 'Yes' to Jesus at each stage.

## SOMEONE UP THERE LOVES YOU (ASCENSION)

Third, I want you to notice that the angels appear again. Luke loves angels, but today I want you to note how often angels bring confusion before they bring clarity. Remember the confusion of Mary when told she's to bear God's Son, before she begins to understand? Remember the turmoil in Peter when heavenly visitors produce the vision of food and challenge him to go and see Cornelius? I wonder whether, at the Ascension, Peter nudges John and says, 'Hey, aren't those the two who were at the empty tomb the other week? What are they doing here?'

What, indeed! The angels are reminding us, every time, that God is doing something fantastic. And we're invited not just to watch it, but to believe it, and then shape and live our lives by it. *'Why stand gazing into heaven?'* say the angels. Is gazing into heaven going to hasten Jesus' return? No! Jesus will come again when he comes. Our job as his disciples is to get on with it. So let's get on with it!

So to three Ascension stories that, together with these three insights help us, I hope, to understand better what the Ascension of Jesus Christ means – the first two of which I can vouch are absolutely true.

As a young man I played in a gospel rock band for several years. It was a rainy autumn evening in October 1976, and our two female singers, Jane and Donna, and I, were travelling to a gig in Summerbridge in my little orange Austin 1300 estate. I swear to this day that I wasn't going very fast, but as I braked for an approaching bend near a village on the moors called Timble, the car skidded on wet leaves, went through a dry stone wall, over a ditch, and crashed into a telegraph pole, which broke and fell onto the roof of the car.

I will never forget the policeman. He came out in the rain. Looked at us, three drowned rats. Looked at the demolished wall. Looked at the telegraph pole. Looked at the car. Looked at the roof so smashed in that it was wedged on the gear lever. Looked at Donna who was ok. Looked at Jane, who had a small gash in her knee, who still has the scar to prove it and has never quite forgiven me. Looked back at the car and said words which I've never forgotten. 'Well, son, somebody up there loves you.'

Now that's what Ascension Day makes clear. It means that someone up there loves you. And when you're down, or crashed out, or devastatingly ill, or out of hope, you'll know just how important it is to know and believe that somebody up there really loves you. Some of us here today need to know that. Somebody up there loves you. He is Lord of heaven and earth. And that's really good news!

Not many miles away from the scene of the wrecked orange Austin 1300 estate is a place called Bewerley Park. It was – still is – an outward-bound centre, and I visited it several times in my teenage years. It was my favourite part of life at school. I loved the canoeing. I adored the potholing. And I hated the climbing.

So, there we were at the bottom of the 'Dancing Bear,' part of Brimham Rocks near Pateley Bridge. The rock face stretched up into the sky. The teacher said to the six of us, 'OK, who's going up first then?' And we all developed a sudden interest in the grass! 'Right,' he said, and began to climb, up and up and out of sight. We waited. Then came a distant shout and a dangled rope appeared. We followed his instructions, attaching the rope on to the carabiner and made our way, one by one, up that almost vertical rock.

I went fifth. Out of six! Just to think of it now nearly fifty years later turns my legs to jelly. How I ever got to the top I'll never know. But I remember all the way the shouts of encouragement. Keeping the rope slack but not too slack, taut but not too taut, but always anchored above. And I recall that quivering, proud feeling as I hauled myself over the top tip of the rock and lay on the grass at the top looking further up into the sky. I remember the claps on the back and the grin of the tutor, 'Well done, lad.' And then said more quietly as he tugged on the rope still attached to me, and to him, and also attached to a huge rock behind us, 'I had you every inch of the way.'

## SOMEONE UP THERE LOVES YOU (ASCENSION)

Now, there was no way on earth that I could've gone up that rock face first. But I did get up that rock following after. There's no way on earth that I can get to heaven on my own. But I can get there following after. And as I seek to be Christ's, he has me every step of the way. That's what the Ascension makes clear.

Finally, there is an old Ascension story that many will know. Jesus re-enters heaven after his Ascension and the Archangel Gabriel bows low. 'Welcome back, my Lord, have you accomplished all you set out to do?' 'I think so,' replies Jesus. 'You've successfully organised a community to carry on your work and teaching?' 'Well,' says Jesus, 'I've left a few people to really get things moving.' 'Only a few!' gasps the archangel, 'Is that all?' 'That's all.' 'These people,' asks the archangel, 'They're people of great importance and scholarship and ability?' 'Not really,' said Jesus, smiling. 'They're just ordinary folk.' 'But my Lord, what if they should fail?' blurts the archangel, 'The whole enterprise will have been in vain. All that cost and suffering will have been wasted.' The reply of Jesus was clear. 'I have made no other plans.'

And we could finish there, but, of course the old story is wrong. It's simply not true that there are no other plans. Or, perhaps better, if not another plan, then at least an all-important dimension of the same plan. For just as the Ascension marks the end of one thing, it marks the beginning of another marvellous act of God. God the Holy Spirit comes and gives words to preach, power to heal, discernment to go and strength to grow. A way is found and another gift of God's self is given. So make sure you're here next week, Pentecost, and we'll talk about the way that's offered, and if sought, given and found.

But for today… do you know that someone up there loves you? Do you know Jesus Christ has gone before you, and following him remains always the best way? Do you know you're part of the post-Ascension plan of God, Father, Son and Holy Spirit? Take courage and go in faith! Amen.

# COME, HOLY SPIRIT

Pentecost Sunday. I've increasingly come to use 'she' to describe the Holy Spirit. Of course God is not male or female in that sense, but as we use 'he' so often I think it right to redress the balance of language a little.

Readings: John 15-17, 25-27 & Acts 2:1-21.

I want to share with you a few things I love about God the Holy Spirit.

First, I love it that the Spirit of God *reveals the truth about Jesus*. Have you ever seen a 'Jesus block'? It's a wood block on which 'Jesus' is put in relief, so it's not immediately apparent what it says.

*Jesus block. M. Atkins*

I remember the first time I saw one on the mantlepiece of Connie, a church member. I couldn't read it at first, and she chuckled at my bewilderment. But when you get it, it's easy! How did we not see it before? Of course it says 'Jesus.' Now that's what the Holy Spirit does for us, she helps us 'get it.' She reveals who Jesus is. (I'll use 'she' in this sermon because although God is strictly neither he or she, many times in Christian history the Spirit has been experienced and portrayed as feminine.)

C. H. Spurgeon, the great 19<sup>th</sup> century Baptist preacher at

London's Metropolitan Tabernacle at the Elephant and Castle, said about the Holy Spirit, 'Behold I saw a dove come from heaven and it alighted upon my shoulder. I turned to look at the dove... so it flew away.' Why did the dove fly away? Because in looking at the dove you'd taken your eyes from Jesus. The Holy Spirit reveals the truth about Jesus. If we get too interested in the Holy Spirit herself, in terms of gifts and charisms, by seeking them for their own sake, or to be thought super-spiritual or especially gifted, then the dove flies away. The Spirit says, in effect, 'I'm not here to be the focus of attention, I'm here to point you to him.' The Holy Spirit reveals who Jesus is, and glorifies him. Will we continue to let the Spirit come to us and work in this way? I hope we're able to say, 'Come, Holy Spirit.'

Second, I love it that the Spirit of God comes alongside us. One of the terms used to describe the Holy Spirit is *paraclete*, a Latinised word from the Greek *parakletos* – '*para*' meaning 'alongside' and '*kletos*' or '*kalein*' meaning 'to call (upon for help).' In Bible translations in English this results in a number of words trying to give expression to *parakletos*. The Holy Spirit is the 'advocate,' 'counsellor,' 'comforter,' 'helper.' '*I will send you another helper,*' says Jesus, '*who will be with you forever.*' The Spirit is God who 'comes alongside,' to help, to console, counsel, to 'be there.' Isn't that wonderful?

I love the way the Spirit of God has been my companion down the years. In the times of greatest joy and the times of deepest sorrow. In the dark nights of the soul. In times of the biggest heartache, and trial and uncertainty. I remember a time I went to speak at a convention many years ago. Like Mr. Wesley, I went 'unwillingly,' driving a long way in torrential rain, wondering what possessed me to say 'Yes' to the invitation a year or so earlier. But also being right in the middle of tests for a then undiagnosed condition, and so knowing something was wrong with me but not knowing just what; knowing I was to have biopsies taken later that week but not knowing what they'd reveal. It was while I was speaking about the Holy Spirit, that I heard myself say something – and in the split second I said it the Spirit said to me, 'Now listen to what you're saying, Martyn, because this is important.'

And I heard myself say this. 'I've come to realise that if I'm unable to continue in active ministry, if I can't preach any more, if I haven't long to live, it won't make a scrap of difference for what God feels about me. Because I'm not valued simply for what I do but for who I am. And I'm a loved child of God.' Now that's the work of the Holy Spirit.

You'll have your own stories of how strength was given, how you made it through. Present stories too, because even now we struggle – often two steps forwards, one step backwards – and the struggle is a long-time part of our life – but we know that the Helper is helping. That without the *paraclete* there'd be no hope at all. The Spirit of God comes alongside us, and although we aren't always as aware of her presence as other times, we know she is with us forever, and for our good. Because God loves us. Whatever else you affirm this Pentecost, affirm that. Speak it to your own heart. 'Come close, come alongside, O Holy Spirit.'

Third, I love it that the Spirit of God is the *Holy* Spirit. And so he leads us gently into holiness. The Spirit bears witness with our spirits that God is speaking, or calling, or desires to work in a new way in our lives. The Holy Spirit enables us, at the deepest recesses of our being to say, 'Yes, Lord.'

When I worked at Cliff College, students used to say to me, 'I feel under conviction.' And I'd say, 'Good!' And they'd say, 'No. That's bad, isn't it?' And I'd say, 'Not necessarily. The Holy Spirit only puts us under conviction of something when God wants to do something about it in our life. It's only bad when we refuse to let God do in us what's necessary to make us more like Christ. When we let the Holy Spirit work in us what's necessary to make us more like Jesus, then conviction is good.' Well, some students 'got it' and some didn't! But notice this. Whenever we're under conviction, or conscious-stricken, or challenged – all things that at the time we often don't like – it actually indicates that God hasn't given up on us. If God had given up on us, we'd just be left alone. On our own. 'I've had it with Atkins,' God would say. 'Never listens. Never obeys. Useless.' But God doesn't do that with me, or you, or any of us. And that's amazing. So the next time you're convicted, or challenged to deeper faith, say to yourself, 'God's not giving up on me and I'm not giving up on me! Come, Holy Spirit.'

I've noticed down the years that there are two essential movements occurring when the Holy Spirit comes to us. The first is *infilling* – and the things I've spoken about so far are about that movement, that action of the Spirit. But the second movement is *outpouring*, and the two movements are intrinsically intertwined. The infilling is related to the outpouring. Because we aren't filled with the Holy Spirit for our own sake, but in order to be and do what God wants of us.

Which leads me to the last thing I love about the Holy Spirit and that is she is constantly leading us into *engagement with God's world and peoples*. Because the Holy Spirit of God is a Spirit of mission. The day of Pentecost isn't so much the birthday of the Church as the birthday of the Christian mission of witness and service. Acts 2 is essentially the story of how frightened people locked in a room, saying their prayers, obediently await the Spirit of God, and the Spirit comes upon them. Tongues of fire alight upon them, and the nearness of God is overwhelming. After the traumas of recent weeks it was just like heaven. It was like lying in a beautiful bath and saying, 'Oh, I could stay here for ever.' And the Spirit comes and pulls the bath plug out and says, 'Well that's a pity because I haven't come just to bless you up, much as I love you. We've got a job to do, now come on.' So the first movement of the Spirit through the apostles is out of the door, into the streets of Jerusalem, and into the crowd, to preach and witness and heal and serve and bless. The real test of Pentecost isn't how much of the Holy Spirit we say we have, but how much the Holy Spirit has of us – all of us, body mind and spirit - placed into the hands of God.

I'm a Wesleyan – sorry, I can't do anything about it! I think that John Wesley's understanding of the Holy Spirit is one of the great gifts of Methodism to the whole Church of Christ. John Wesley talked of the prevenient work of the Spirit – the 'going-beforeness' of God. A big Holy Spirit, who within the Trinity of God loves and infuses the world just as God in Christ loved the world and died to save it. Which is why the brooding, wooing, convicting, converting work of the Holy Spirit is to be found everywhere. The Spirit is the Spirit of life. All life.

Anyone who's watched *The Apprentice* will know the famous words of Alan Sugar – 'You're fired.' It means you're being rejected. You've failed and you're out. That's not the way of God's Holy Spirit. But there is one similarity. The Spirit does say to us, 'You're fired.' She says, 'You're burned through, with divine love and power. I'll continue to reveal the Lord Jesus to you. I'll continue to be alongside you, so that you might know ever more of him. I'll continue to convict you and lead you towards holiness, because I love you. But I fill you too, in order that you be people of outpouring into the world I love, a gift to every soul for whom the Lord Jesus died!

*Fire. H. Atkins*

So don't be surprised, when you say, 'Come Holy Spirit' and the Spirit comes, that the first thing she says to you is, 'Come with me.' And at that point we'll understand better what Pentecost is about. Amen.

# 38

# SAINTS AND SOULS REVISITED

Preached on the Sunday after Halloween, All Saints Day and All Souls Day.

Readings: Psalm 46, Hebrews 12:1-6 & John 15:8-13.

Recent days have been a mixture of sacred and secular commemorations. Three days ago was Halloween – 'All Hallows' Eve' – the evening before the holy ones are remembered. It's curious that it should become associated with what it now is. Then came All Saints Day, when we give thanks to God for the great and the good of Christianity, stretching down the ages, around the world,

*Light tunnel at Kew Gardens. H. Atkins*

and up to heaven. 'For all the Saints, who from their labours rest,' and all that. Then yesterday was All Souls Day. Which has dubious origins for Christians of the Reformation, who've never thought much of praying for the dead and even less of giving alms so they might be released from purgatory more quickly than otherwise.

Better, on All Souls Day, is the remembering of the faithful who have died, those 'ordinary' Christian souls who have influenced and shaped our lives for good, saints with a small 's' but no less important to us. Souls.

I want to focus upon saints *and* souls today. Not just the stained-glass window saints, but all the souls who sought to live as Christian disciples, like you and I. Souls who've helped us on our spiritual journey, souls who've been saints to us! More specifically, I want to speak about some characteristics of saints and souls alike – of both 'special' Christians and 'ordinary' Christians – if there is such a thing!

First, saints and souls believe that *selflessness rather than selfishness* is the way of Christ. Many historic saints and souls wouldn't recognise much of today's spirituality as anything other than innately selfish. 'It's all about you,' they'd say. 'It's all on your terms. It's all conditioned by whether you get something out of it or not.' And I guess in a cultural context characterised by consumerism and choice it's sadly inevitable that this drips into the life of the Spirit.

How significant then that saints and souls alike are those who, like John the Baptist say, 'He must increase... and I must decrease.' That's a strange challenge for many of us today, but I have a hunch the ancients knew better than we the kind of life which pleases God. Each year at our covenant service we Methodists say, 'I am no longer my own, but yours.' As Jesus said, 'If you want to keep your life, then give it away.' Through constant battles with self, and circumstance, and conscience, and feeling taken for granted, and misunderstood, and unblessed, continue to offer your life for God's use and place yourself into God's keeping.

Now this may sound all a bit too downbeat, too low-key, with not enough daring-do and dragons – you know, the stuff of proper saints. But not a bit of it. To live such a life is full of challenge and courage.

Second, saints and souls *let God use whichever bit of them God wants.*

Of the many wonderful sights in Budapest, one of the more modest is a building which looks out of place. It looks British and like a school, and it is situated in an area where all surrounding buildings look more... Hungarian! The building looks like a British school because that's what it was. The Church of Scotland built it and schooled both Gentile and Jewish children together for many years. Jewish children because Budapest, in the early decades of the 20th century, was home to one of the largest populations of Jews in Europe. At least a quarter of a million Jews lived there prior to the Second World War and because of the inhumane things that then happened, far fewer survived. But I leap ahead of myself.

One of the matrons at the school was Jane Haining. She'd worked there since 1932. But there came a time when the dark clouds of the Third Reich loomed and the Church of Scotland called their staff home – just like some aid agencies are doing this very day. Jane Haining refused. She no doubt said something like, 'How can I leave these children when now is the time when more than ever I must remain with them?' So she stayed, and in a situation few of us can even imagine, ran the school in war time, in Budapest, caring for both Jewish and Gentile children alike. She hid Jewish children – like Oskar Schindler – in families all over the city. She was arrested in 1944 and died in Auschwitz-Birkenau alongside those she loved and cared for.

Now that itself makes her something of a saint in my eyes, but again I leap ahead of myself. Because as a woman from a well-to-do Scottish family she'd been raised to run a large house. She knew how to lead, to manage people, to organise, plan and plant. Indeed it was this very genteel lifestyle that she felt God was calling her away from when, no doubt to the dismay of her parents, she went as a missionary, a lowly matron, to a place like Hungary.

229

And yet. And yet it was the very things she felt she'd left behind in order to serve God that became the things that most enabled her to do what God wanted. You see, sometimes a bit of your life which seems unimportant and peripheral takes centre stage in God's plans for you. So being a saint or a soul isn't only about the religious bits of our lives. It's about all of us. Every part. You'll have areas of your lives you think God isn't interested in, or you think are peripheral to the business of being Christian. If so, you're wrong. It's all included. It may be your work, the way you spend your time, the way you treat those nearest to you, how you are with your friends, your special gifts and talents. Or you may have that all-too-common Christian disorder, the SSD – Sacred/Secular Divide – where you've chosen which are the sacred bits of life and which are the secular bits of life, and you keep them well apart. God is involved with one and not the other, you think. But saints and souls are those who let God use every bit of them, even those pieces which they think are outside or redundant to God's purposes.

Just one more thing. Saints and souls *strive to be hope-full even when it's tempting to be hopeless.*

I remember many years ago interviewing Fiona Castle, the wife of the celebrity entertainer Roy Castle, a few months after his untimely death. It was a moving occasion. She was in tears, I was in tears, and most of the several hundred people in the auditorium were in tears. I asked her, 'Given what's happened to Roy and to you,' – which had clearly ripped her life apart at that time – 'how are you able to bear Christian testimony on occasions like this?' And she talked about her trust in the love and the keeping of God, and the times she doubted it in the dead of night, but somehow, someway, clung to the love that would not let her go. Then she said, 'Roy would want me to keep faith. I see him in a huge arena, like an Olympic stadium, with thousands of others who've gone before us, and he's by the finishing line and shouting encouragement to me, "Come on girl, you can do it!"' You can imagine why there wasn't a dry eye in the house!

But you see she's right. That's what the writer to the Hebrews is talking about when talking of the great cloud of witnesses. They're not taking bets on our failure, they're willing us on.

But there's a still deeper hope which, when all else appears stripped away, remains firm. You see the Holy Spirit is given to us to run the race, to enable us to say 'Yes' when without the Spirit we could say only 'No.' The One who is alongside us, and within us, willing us to God's will, making possible those things that without the Holy Spirit would be impossible. So that when the saints and souls in the cloud of witnesses urge us on, the Holy Spirit bears witness with our spirits and says, 'Yes.' Because the resourcing of saints and souls alike isn't so much about how much of the Holy Spirit they've got, but how much the Holy Spirit has got them! And in the end, that's what defines both God's saints and God's souls. As John Wesley said as he went to be with his Lord, and ours, 'The best of all is, God is with us.' Amen.

**Other books by Martyn Atkins include:**

*Resourcing Renewal: Shaping Churches for the Emerging Future*
*Discipleship and the People Called Methodists*
*Sermon on the Mount: Following Jesus in Today's World*
*Preaching in a Cultural Context*

Martyn has contributed to over twenty further titles.

.